LECTURES

ON

THE EPISTLE OF JUDE

LECTURES
ON
THE EPISTLE OF JUDE

(TRANSLATED FROM A CORRECTED TEXT)

BY

W. KELLY

NEW EDITION
REVISED BY W. J. HOCKING.

BELIEVERS BOOKSHELF
P.O. Box 261
Sunbury, Pennsylvania 17801

PRINTED IN THE UNITED STATES OF AMERICA—1970

CONTENTS

LECTURES ON
THE EPISTLE OF JUDE

INTRODUCTION

WE are arrived at those days now of which the
Epistle of Jude speaks. I might say we are further,
for the Epistles of John, although they are put before
this Epistle, imply from their own contents that they
were after. The order of the books in the N.T., we
know is entirely human, and, in fact, is not the same
in all Bibles. In English ones it is, but abroad it is
not so, and in the more ancient copies of the Scriptures there was another order, in some respects even
less correct than that which we have ; because these
Epistles of Jude and John are put before the Epistles
of Paul. I need not say that there was no divine
wisdom in that. I only mention it for the purpose of
emphasising the absolute need of the guidance of
the Holy Spirit. It is no matter what it is. The people
in early days, it might have been thought, would
have had a good sound judgment of how to arrange
the books of Holy Scripture, but they had not. I
am speaking now of a time long after the apostles,
and we are still more distant. But we are at no
disadvantage because of this, for the reason that the
Holy Ghost Who was given, still abides. The ruin of

the church does not affect that gift. It is a very solemn fact, and it does greatly bear upon the practical answer of the church to the glory of the Lord Jesus, and it makes not a small difference for the members of Christ. But the Lord provided for everything when He sent down the Holy Spirit ; and He made known through the apostles that this was the sad history which awaited the church. It is the apostles who tell us what disasters were to flow in with a strong tide—nobody more so than the apostle Paul, who says, " I know that after my decease shall grievous wolves enter in among you, not sparing the flock." Oh, what characters ! What successors ! Apostolic successors !—there are none. The successors were to be grievous wolves and perverse men. Nevertheless, he commended the saints none the less confidently " to God and to the word of His grace."

Well, we have this ; and I do not think that the word of His grace has ever been so deeply enjoyed, as it is now, for many hundreds of years. But then, Who is it that enjoys the " word of His grace " ? We cannot say that all the saints do. All saints ought to do. Can we say that all our dear brethren and sisters enjoy the word of His grace as it becomes them ? I would to God it were so ; and it is of all moment therefore that, knowing the need, we should be most earnest not merely about work—I allow that this has a great place for all true workers, and I admit that many can help the workers who are not

exactly workers themselves—but, beloved friends,
the first of all duties is that God should have His
rights. This is forgotten, even by saints of God. The
first-fruits belong to Him always, it does not matter
what it is ; and we are never right when it is merely
love working outwardly. The first thing is that love
should work upward. Is not God infinitely more to
us than any converts—as could be said to poor
Naomi, who had lost her sons—" better to thee than
seven sons " ? Is not He worth more than a hundred
thousand converts ? What a poor thing it is, merely
to be useful to other people and not to be growing
ourselves in grace, and in the knowledge of our Lord
Jesus Christ ! How can this be done except by God
and the word of His grace ? How does God act now ?
By His Spirit. Time was when the great truth was
God manifesting Himself by His Son. Well, that
abides ; the word and Spirit of God abide for ever.
But now the Holy Ghost is sent down from heaven.
He is that divine Person with Whom we have to do
habitually, and we are either honouring Him, or
failing to do so. The great test of honouring Him is
that Christ becomes all. This is a truth that got
greatly clouded even in apostolic days. It may be a
very small comfort; it is a very solemn and sadden-
ing comfort, too, if I may use such a conjunction of
thoughts, but so it is when we think how everything
tends to failure and towards decline, not excepting the
testimony of God which was committed to His children.

It is a very solemn thing that the apostles had the

very same experiences themselves. The last of them had to face the fact that the very best of the churches —that which had been the brightest—became the object of the Lord's warning, and the last of the churches of the Lord's threatening ; a warning of what soon came to pass, and a threatening to be surely executed viz.—to take away the candlestick of the one, and to spue the other out of His mouth (Rev. ii., iii.).

Now, is that meant to weaken confidence ? It was revealed in order to enforce the need of dependence upon the Lord, to encourage us to look up from the earth and things that are here—but not to give up. We are never free to give up anything that is of God. We are never at liberty to plead the state of ruin for carelessness about any expression of God's will. The ruin of the church has nothing to do with weakening our responsibility. It brings in the necessity of greater watchfulness, of more prayer ; and particularly the necessity of God and the word of His grace to deal with the difficulties altogether above man. But are they above the Spirit of God ?

Now, it is in this very spirit that Jude writes— " a servant of Jesus Christ." For he does not appear to have been the apostle Jude. Most take it for granted that it was only an apostle wrote this or any of the Epistles. This is a mistake. Many of the apostles never wrote any inspired writing, and some that were not apostles wrote both Gospels and Epistles. It is a question of inspiration, a question of a particular work of God, of which vessel the Holy

Ghost would use. Out of the four who wrote the
Gospels, two were apostles, and two were not
apostles ; so with the Epistles, as it appears to me,
for I should not wish to press a thing that is so very
much doubted by many persons. But then it is well
to remember that almost everything is doubted
now-a-days !

It is of interest to consider who is speaking to us
in this Epistle. We are told it is " Jude, servant
of Jesus Christ and brother of James." He is not
the brother of James the son of Zebedee—John was
his brother. That James was cut off from very early
days indeed, and John was left latest of all ; so
different was the issue for these two sons of Zebedee.
There was another James (as also another Jude or
Judas, besides the Iscariot), " son of Alphæus," who
is named " James the Little " (Mark xv. 40). I
do not think that this is the James referred to here,
but rather that he is the one who has been called
" James the Just " ; and I presume that this title
was given to him because of his practical pre-
eminence. He was a hater of evil and a lover of all
that was morally pleasing to God. He comes before
us too, in Acts xv., though not for the first time
there. In that chapter he takes a great place. He,
as far as one can so say, presided, and that is a
very proper scripture word. Those " that rule well "
means those that preside well. There is nothing
wrong in presiding if a man can do it ; it is a mistake
if a man cannot, and assumes to do it ; and it is

one of the worst things possible when done now by
an official, whether there is power or not. But there
is such a thing as "ruling" or "presiding"
recognised, though it is never confined to one person,
"them that have the rule (or, preside) over you"
(Heb. xiii. 17) : there we have several.

But we are not anxious about the matter. One
might be more prominent on one day, another on
another day, but James seems to have been prominent habitually, and this appears to have been quite
recognised by the elders at Jerusalem. We find Paul
going up to see James, and all the elders were present
(Acts xx. 18). This is the man who wrote the
Epistle, who also calls himself "a servant of . . .
Jesus Christ." Of course, this is true of all, and is
said by almost all. The apostle Paul calls himself
that continually, and of course so do Peter and John,
although the latter calls himself "the disciple
whom Jesus loved" rather, but still he calls himself
a servant of Jesus Christ in the Revelation (i. 2)—
"to His servant John." So you see that it is only a
question of the propriety of the case where this word
is put forward ; and it certainly was very appropriate
in the book of the Revelation, and there accordingly
it is. Elsewhere, in his Gospel especially, John dwells
rather on the Saviour's love, and in that book he
does not call himself anything. We only know by
internal evidence that he must be the man whom he
describes, not as John, but, as "the disciple whom
Jesus loved."

But James was not a " disciple " ; he was one
of the Lord's brethren who did not believe all the
time the Lord was living here below ; " neither did
His brethren believe on Him " (John vii. 5). " His
brethren " were sons of Mary after His own birth.
Of course we can understand that Romanists have
been anxious to make out that they were sons of
Joseph and not of Mary. But they were sons of
Mary and of Joseph. They would like to make
them out sons of a former marriage of Joseph. We
do not know anything of a former marriage, nor do
they. We do know that scripture is quite plain.

Take Mark vi. 3 for instance, and there you will
find that what I have just stated is fully acknowledged : speaking of our Lord, it says, " Is not
this the carpenter the son of Mary, and brother "
(not the cousin, you see) " of James and Joses, and
of Juda and Simon ? " We do not know what
particular place God gave to Joses and Simon, but
we do know that James and Judas, or Jude (it is
the same name), were both called to an eminent
service.

Now if we look at the first of Acts we get more. It
appears there were sisters also, but we need not
now pursue that subject. In Acts i. 13 we read,
" And when they " (*i.e.* the apostles) " were come in,
they went up into an upper room, where abode both
Peter and James " (that James is the son of Zebedee),
" and John " (his brother), " and Andrew, Philip
and Thomas, Bartholomew and Matthew, James

[the son] of Alphæus " (that is, James the Little)
" and Simon Zelotes " (to distinguish him from
Simon Peter and from Simon the Lord's brother),
" and Judas [the brother] of James."

Now, in my judgment, the last two names are
brought before us in the opening verse of our
Epistle, " Jude, the servant of Jesus Christ, and
brother of James." But we further read in the same
chapter of the Acts, " These all continued with one
accord in prayer and supplication, with the women,
and Mary the mother of Jesus, and with his brethren"
(ver. 14). Who these " brethren " are, we have
already seen from Mark vi. James and Jude were
two of the Lord's brethren. Simon and Joses were
two others. But we do not need to dwell on these,
because Scripture does not do so. Yet it says a deal
about James ; not so much about Jude. As already
noticed, although they were unconverted all the
time the Lord was on earth they were evidently
converted after the Lord died and rose ; so that there
they were with Mary their mother, and the eleven,
all living together and given up to prayer, and
waiting for the promise of the Father, the gift of the
Holy Spirit. It is certain they were not unconverted
now. Nothing would have been more contrary to
their mind had they not been believers, but now
they are believers for the first time. And very beautiful it is to see that God broke them down by the
very thing that might have stumbled them for ever.
The crucifying of the Lord might have entirely

hindered, but God used that and the Lord's resurrection, not only to awaken their souls, but to bring
them in, so that they were there, full of the same
expectation of the Holy Ghost as the apostles themselves.

Consequently, when James, the son of Zebedee,
was killed (Acts xii.), we find another James, who is
not described as the son of Alphæus, and who is the
one that has evidently stepped forward, by God's
guidance, into a kind of foremost place. For when
all the apostles were there, Peter and John amongst
the rest, they did not take that place, much less
any other of the twelve. James did, and to show you
that I am not incorrect in this, I will give you
another scripture, (Galatians i. 15–19), which is very
convincing and satisfactory. The apostle Paul is
showing how he had been kept from mixing up with
any other of the apostles in particular, at the time
he was brought to the knowledge of the Lord Jesus.
" But when it pleased God, Who separated me from
my mother's womb, and called [me] by His grace,
to reveal His Son in me, that I might preach Him
among the heathen ; immediately I conferred not
with flesh and blood ; neither went I up to Jerusalem
to them which were apostles before me ; but I went
into Arabia, and returned again unto Damascus.
Then after three years, I went up to Jerusalem to
see Peter, and abode with him fifteen days. But
other of the apostles saw I none, save James, the
Lord's brother " (not the Lord's " cousin ").

Apparently, James, the son of Alphæus, was the Lord's cousin. Now we all know that the word " brother " is sometimes used loosely, but in that case it is always corrected by some other parts of scripture. But this is not corrected by any ; and I do not see any reason why—if the Spirit of God calls Mark, not exactly the nephew, but cousin of Barnabas (the word there used is " cousin "),— James should not be so called here, if he were not really the " brother " of our Lord.

It is true James does not call himself " the Lord's brother," but " the Lord's servant " ; and this is very beautiful. Had there been any self-seeking he would have been the one to say, " I am the Lord's brother ! You must not forget I am the Lord's brother." But that would have been anything but of the Spirit of God, because when he was the Lord's brother, he was an unbeliever. He had been an un-believer during all the life of our Lord. Indeed, he was so until His death and resurrection. He, there-fore, with beautiful grace, never brings up that which was his shame—that he was the Lord's brother after the flesh. The Lord Himself put all that sort of thing down, when He declared that it was not so much the blessed thing to be the woman that bare Him, as it was to hear the word of God and keep it. This is what the writer of this Epistle had done ; he had heard the word of God and kept it. He had received the truth of Christ's Person not as son of Mary but as the Son of God, as the Messiah, the Lord

of all. Here then Jude was glad to say, not that he
was the Lord's brother, though he was so, but, " a
servant of Jesus Christ," and he adds, to make it
perfectly clear who he was, " brother of James."

So we have here the plain fact that this James
was not the son of Zebedee, who had been killed
many years before ; neither was he James the little.
We may call him rather, James the great, because
he takes such a foremost place wherever mentioned.
Acts xv. puts it in a very striking manner which I
had better not pass over. After Peter had given his
very important testimony, and Paul and Barnabas
their evidence, about the reception of the Gentiles,
we come to another person (ver. 13) , " James
answered, saying." You see the others are regarded
as speaking, but James answers, " Men, brethren "
(that is the proper way to read it ; " and " has nothing to do with it). They were not merely men, but
men who were brethren. " Men, brethren, hearken
unto me. Simon hath declared how God at the first
did visit the Gentiles, to take out of them a people
for His name . . . Wherefore my sentence is . . ."
(vers. 13-19). No one can doubt the place that he
took, and that the Spirit of God sanctions his taking
it. James was the one who, after having heard all
the facts, summed up the mind of God, and quoted
a decisive scripture. And this is a very interesting
thing that, though they were inspired men, they did
not do without the scriptures. When you have facts
in the light of scripture, you are then entitled to draw

therefrom the truth—what he calls here "my sentence," and what was written in the nineteenth and following verses.

The other striking place where James appears is in Acts xxi. where Paul goes up to Jerusalem. "And the day following "—that is after the arrival— "Paul went in with us to James; and all the elders were present" (ver. 18). It is evident that this was the great central place of meeting for strangers at Jerusalem, and that the elders also were accustomed to be present on those occasions. These facts give it evidently a very official character, which was perfectly compatible with the position of James at Jerusalem. Tradition makes him the bishop of the church in Jerusalem, but scripture never speaks of " the " bishop, but of " bishops " : and scripture also shows that there were more important persons than the bishops ; and James had a place of evident superiority to any of the " elders " (these were the bishops), a place that none of the elders possessed to the same degree. And this James is the one that wrote the Epistle that bears his name, as that of Jude was written by his brother.

It is instructive to see how God allowed the unbelief of the family of our Lord Jesus. It was not like people plotting together. If you look at the great leader of the Eastern apostasy, Mahomet, it was so. His family were persons whom he induced to take their place along with him, to defend him and stand by him. But in the case of our Lord Jesus Christ,

God allowed that His own brethren should not believe
on Him all the time that His mighty works were
being done. But there was another work, the greatest
of all, and God made that work irresistible. Not
indeed the works of His life, but that of His death and
resurrection ; and these brethren that had stood
out so stubbornly against Him were brought out to
believe on Him through His work of sin bearing.
There was a reason for their unbelief. There are
always moral causes, which act particularly in
unconverted persons to prevent their reception of
the truth. Sometimes it is the fleshly mind, sometimes the worldly mind, sometimes both. In the
case of these brethren, their worldly mind came out
strongly in John vii. 4, 5, when they said, " If Thou
do these things, show Thyself to the world. For
neither did His brethren believe on Him." The Lord
was infinitely far from doing this. He was not of the
world, and tells us we are not. He never sought the
world in any form. He only sought to do good to souls
in it by delivering them out of the world to make
them know the true God, and Himself equally the
true God and Life eternal.

Well now, we have this fact so full of interest—
that James gives us, according to the spiritual
character that was formed in him, a most complete
setting forth of practical righteousness in everyday
life, in our tempers, in our words, as well as our ways.
All this is unfolded by James more than by any
other, and it is only from want of understanding it,

that some do not like his Epistle. Sometimes great
and good men have kicked at the plainness of speech
in James. They have not liked it ; but it was a
great loss to them, for had they heeded what he
wrote it would have corrected many a fault in themselves.

Now in Jude there is another subject altogether.
Righteousness is not the point in Jude ; not even
the way in which Peter brings it in. Jude does not
look at it for personal walk simply, apart from the
ruin of those that give it up. He merely shows
righteousness to be a necessary thing for every saint.
If a man has not got it, he is not a saint at all. But
Peter in his Second Epistle looks at it in a large way
among the people of God—whether they as His
people walk righteously, and more particularly
whether the teachers are indifferent to righteousness
and are favouring unrighteousness. Therefore his
Second Epistle is levelled most strongly at these—
the false teachers who, not content with being
personally so themselves, encourage others to similar
lack of righteousness. Now, this is not what Jude
takes up at all, though there is much that is common
to them both. It could not be otherwise.

Jude looks at grace. There is nothing like grace ;
but what if grace be abused ? What if grace be
abandoned ? What if grace be turned to licentiousness ? Now that is what Jude takes up. Consequently, his Epistle is one of the most solemn in the
word of God. There is only one writer who is more

so—John. John looks at not merely the departure
from grace, but the denial of Christ, of the Father
and the Son. Well, it is impossible to conceive of
anything worse in scripture than denying the glory
of Him unto Whose name I may have been baptised,
and through Whom I have professed to receive
every blessing that God could give. After all that,
for a man to be induced by his intellect, or from
whatever cause, to deny the Lord, to deny that He
was the Christ and the Son of God—there is nothing
more deadly—there is nothing more terrible than
the state of such a one. And it fell to the lot of him
who loved the Lord most, to John, to write about
this denial. So that you see that there is a beautiful
propriety in all the Epistles.

VERSE I

" JUDE, servant of Jesus Christ, and brother of
James, to them that are (not exactly, ' sanctified,'
but) beloved." This may surprise many who have
been accustomed to the Authorised Version, but it
is not a question of what we have been accustomed
to, but of what God wrote. The Authorised Version
is an admirable one. Our translators did not mistake the meaning of the Greek word in the text
before them ; but the text which they had was the
common text, and this text is as faulty in its way as
the common English Version. This text was tran-

scribed by a number of different hands, and if the
writing was not very clear there was always a ten-
dency for the copyist to make mistakes.

I have had a deal of writing pass through my
hands, but I hardly have seen any, where there is
not some mistake made.   Particularly when the
writing is a copy of another, it is almost always so,
and more particularly when the man whose thoughts
and words are copied is above the common people.
The way to find out the best Greek text is to go up
to the oldest of all, and to compare the oldest of all
with the different translations made in ancient times,
and if these agree, then you have the right one. But
they often disagree, and then comes the question,
Which is right ?   Here the all important question is
the guidance of the Spirit of God. We can never do
without Him, and the way in which the Spirit of
God leads persons who really are not only indwelt
by Him, but led by Him, is,—does it express the
current of the Epistle ? Does it fall in with the line
of the apostle's writing ?

Well, you see the word " sanctified " may be
correct in itself, but the word here should be, " to
those that are called, beloved," etc. You observe
that the word " called " occurs at the end of the
verse. This word " called " is very emphatic. Then
he describes them in two different ways. First, here,
in the A.V., it is " sanctified," but as now generally
accepted by those who have studied the text fully, it

is " beloved* in God the Father." " In " is very
often equivalent to (indeed, it is a stronger expression
that) " by." But I now give it literally, " beloved
in God the Father." I confess myself that not only
is this reading the most ancient, the best approved
by the highest witnesses that God has given to us of
His word, but it is beautifully appropriate to the
Epistle. The assurance of being " beloved in God
the Father," or " by God the Father," comes
into special value under two sets of circumstances.
If I am a young man very young in the faith, when
one is proving the persecution of the world, the
hatred of men, Jews full of jealousy, the Gentiles
full of scorn, and both animated by hatred against
the Lord and those that are the Lord's—what a
comfort it is to know that I am beloved " in God the
Father." This is the way the apostle Paul addressed
the Thessalonians as a company, the only one that
he ever addressed in this way. They were experienc-
ing persecution, not in a gradual way as most of the
other assemblies had done, but from the very start,
from their conversion. We know the apostle himself
had to flee because of the persecution that had set
in there. " These men that have turned the world
upside down have come here also," and a deadly set
was made upon them, and so the apostle had to
escape. The church there had to bear the brunt of it,
and in the very first Epistle that Paul ever wrote, the

---

* ἠγαπημένοις (beloved) ℵAB and several cursives, all the Ancient
Versions, Origen, &c. ἠγιασμένοις (sanctified) KLP &c.

First to the Thessalonians—that was his first inspired writing—you will find that such is the manner in which he describes them. " Paul and Silvanus and Timotheus to the assembly of Thessalonians in God [the] Father and [the] Lord Jesus Christ " (1 Thess. ii. 1). And that this was studiously meant is shown by the same presentation of the truth in the opening verse of the Second Epistle, where we find there was still the persecution and the danger of their being shaken by that persecution and the error that had come in through false teachers taking advantage of it to pretend that " the day of the Lord " was actually on them, making out that this persecution was the beginning of that " day," and so greatly alarming the young believers there.

Hence the apostle had to write a second letter to establish them clearly in the bright hope of Christ's coming, and in the lower truth of the day of the Lord. Well, in that Second Epistle we have " Paul and Silvanus and Timotheus to the assembly of Thessalonians in God our Father and [the] Lord Jesus Christ " (2 Thess. ii. 1). Now I conceive that the object of the Spirit of God there, by the apostle, was, that as they were so young and so exposed to such an assault upon themselves, which reminded the apostle of the assault which had been made upon himself and his friends, that they should be comforted by the reminder that they were " in God the Father." What could harm them if this were the case ? The apostle would not have ventured from

himself to say such a thing. None upon earth would
have done so. It was God Who inspired the apostle
to let them know that wonderful comfort. There
are many people who read this and do not get any
comfort from it, because they do not apply it to
themselves. They have no idea what it means. You
will remember that John, writing in his First
Epistle, separates the family of God into three classes
—the fathers, young men and the babes (for I give
the last word as it should be, literally). They are
all " children " of God, but the babes are the young
ones of the children of God. The young men are those
that have grown up, and the fathers are those that
are mature and well established in Christ. Well,
it is to the babes—and this will help us to understand what I have been saying—he says, " I write
unto you babes " (the proper full force of the word),
" because ye have known the Father " (1 John ii.
13).

Well, so it is with this young assembly in Thessal-
onica. It is described by the Holy Ghost as being
" in God [the] Father and in [the] Lord Jesus Christ."

In Jude we have the other side. They are not
young saints now. It is addressed to comparatively
old saints. There might be young ones among them ;
there would be such, undoubtedly. But he is looking
at them as having gone through a sea of trouble and
difficulty, and he is preparing them for worse still.
He, as it were, says things are not going to get better
but worse, and it is to end in the actual appearing

of the Lord in judgment, and what is more, the very kind of people who are to be the objects of the Lord's judgment when He comes have crept into the church already. This is a very solemn thing, and it might be alarming unless people were well read and grounded in the truth, and in love. So, therefore, writing at a comparatively late time (not early as in the case of the Thessalonians, but late), Jude writes in these terms—" to them that are called." You observe that I transpose that word, which is a little spoiled by the interpolation of the conjunction " and " before " called." " To them that are called, beloved in God the Father, and preserved." It is not exactly " preserved *in*." It may be " by " or " for." These are the two alternatives for that word. I do not see how it can be " in " ; so that you see it little differs from what we read here. It brings in another idea, and it is perfectly true either way. We are preserved *by* Christ, and we are preserved *for* Christ. I have not made up my mind which of the two in this instance is right, because they cannot both be the intention of the Spirit of God. One must be right rather than the other, but I cannot say that my judgment is yet formed as to the choice of these two prepositions, whether it should be " preserved for Jesus Christ," or " by " Jesus Christ, He being the great One that does keep us. But in either case, how beautifully it is suited to a time of extra danger, and of danger too that he was not warranted to say would pass ! We say the storm

rages now, but the sun will shine shortly. No ; it is
to be that blackness of darkness of evil which is now
coming in among the professors of Christ to get
denser and darker until the Lord comes in judgment
on them.

Well, how sweet is the assurance, " beloved in
God the Father, and preserved by (or for) Jesus
Christ " (either way is full of brightness—and the
Lord may give us to learn some day which of the two
thoughts is His meaning). But there it is, and full of
comfort and sweetness, and eminently suited to the
circumstances portrayed in this Epistle beyond any
Epistle in the New Testament—an Epistle that
shows the departure of Christians, i.e., of professing
Christians—of those who were once thought to be
as good as any. Sometimes, the people who turn
away are those that have been very bright. We
should not be surprised at that. It is not always the
best fruit that ripens most quickly. Sometimes
the earliest becomes rotten very soon. This is often
the case with those that seem so bright all at once.

I remember being struck with this in the case of a
young woman in the Isle of Wight, some forty years
ago. Charles Stanley, our dear brother, in his zeal
for the gospel was somewhat in danger of fancying
people were converted when they were not. At times
of revival, people are often apt to slip in ; their
feelings are moved, they are quickly affected.
According to the word in the Gospel, " they hear the
word, and anon with joy receive it ; yet have they

no root in themselves, but endure for a while : for when trial or persecution arises because of the word, immediately they are offended " (Matt. xiii. 20, 21) ; so that we ought not to be surprised. The young woman of whom I speak was employed in a shop, and I was brought to see her as one of these conversions. In a moment she assured me that the old man was all gone, " dead and buried," and other such language she used. This would have been all very sweet had there been any real spiritual feeling ; but she had merely caught the truth in her mind, at best.

Now, a real convert having confessed the truth of Christ for the first time, would be greatly tried by many things, failings, shortcomings, and the like. The soul of such a one would be greatly alarmed to think that, even after having received Christ, he found so little that answered to His love, so easily betrayed into levity or carelessness, or into haste of temper, and ever so many difficulties that a young believer is tried by. But the young woman of whom I have been speaking had no conscience about anything at all. All she had was merely an intellectual idea of the truth that seemed delightful to her, and, indeed, it is delightful. It is like those described in Heb. vi. 5, they " have tasted the good word of God," and there they are, " enlightened " by the great light of the gospel, without being truly born of God. There might be a powerful action of the Spirit of God, and there may be all this without

being truly born of God. People who are really born
of God are generally tried, and there is a great
sense of sin, and they have to learn their powerless-
ness. All this is a very painful experience ; and it is
to this state that the comfort of the gospel applies
the knowledge of entire forgiveness and clearance
from all that we are ; not only in spite of what we
are, but because of what we are, because of all that
God has given us—a new life where there is no sin.
There never is anything like this true comfort except
in those that have felt the need of it, and that
sense of need is what goes along with conversion to
God. The Old Testament saints were in that state ;
and they never got out of it. The New Testament
saints began with conversion and came into blessing
that was impossible with the law—because the
mighty work of redemption was not done. But now
it is done ; and can we suppose it does not make an
essential difference for a New Testament believer ?
Well ! " if any man be ignorant, let him be ignorant." Here you have this invaluable comfort for
those that have passed through such serious experiences and who have proved their own weakness in
meeting it—the liability to be affected by appearances which come to nothing. Fair and smooth words
where there is no reality at all—this is what is so
trying. And the Epistle shows that people are going
to get worse than this.

VERSES 2, 3

THEN (ver. 2) we have, " mercy unto you, and peace and love be multiplied." This is the only place where mercy is wished to the saints generally. When writing to individuals, to Timothy and Titus, for instance, the apostle says " Mercy," but when to the saints generally, " Grace and peace."

Why does Jude bring " mercy " in here ? Because they deeply needed the comfort. An individual ought always to feel the deep need of mercy, especially in the face of danger, and also in the sense of personal unworthiness ; and now Jude gives the comfort of it to all these saints because of their imminent danger. I do not know any saints more in danger than ourselves, because grace has given us to feel for Christ's honour and name, and to have confidence in the scriptures as the word of God. We should not look at a single word in them as a dead letter. I do not suppose that there is a single person here present—brother or sister—that has a doubt of a single word that God has written. It would be difficult now-a-days to find yourself in such a company generally. People think inspiration is a very lively term, and that we must allow for the errors of those good men who wrote the Bible. What could we expect from such men even if learned? They judge by themselves, not by God, nor by the Holy Ghost. Many of these men have not, I think, abandoned Christianity ; but they are darkened by

the spirit of unbelief. The spirit of the present day
is as bad or worse as in any age since the Lord died
and rose. There is one thing that marks it, and, that
is lawlessness. A want of respect for everything
that is above self, and a determination to have one's
own way—that is lawlessness. I do not know anything worse. It is what will characterise the whole
of Christendom. Now it works in individuals, and it
also works largely in whole companies, but it will
soon become the reigning spirit. And that is the
distinctive name of the anti-christ, " the lawless
one." Christ was the Man of righteousness, Christ
is the Man that gives everything its place according
to God, and Christ is the One that gives God His
place. As to everything and every person, He was the
Man of righteousness ; lawlessness has nothing but
self as its great ambition, a fallen self—man fallen
from God. The danger is great in the present day,
and so it was when Jude wrote his Epistle. Therefore
it is " mercy," not only " peace and love," but
" mercy " be multiplied. It is a very emphatic word.

" Beloved, when I gave all diligence to write
unto you of the common salvation, it was needful
for me to write unto you, and exhort that ye should
earnestly contend for the faith which was once
delivered to the saints " (ver. 3). It is addressed to
those that have learned the value of " the faith."
He does not refer to personal faith but to the deposit
that the faith holds. It is the thing believed, not
merely the spiritual power that believes the testi-

mony. It is therefore called "the faith," distinct from "faith." When did that faith come? The Epistle to the Galatians shows us when faith came and redemption and the Holy Ghost. It is found in iii. 25 : "For after that faith is come." "I live by the faith of the Son of God." ; "Received ye the Spirit by the hearing of faith? " is a distinct thing (ii.20 ; iii. 2). "The scripture hath concluded all under sin" (Jews or Gentiles—the Jews under transgression, but *all* under sin) "that the promise by faith of Jesus Christ might be given to them that believe. But before faith came we were kept under law," (iii. 22, 23). The law was there until the cross of Christ, but then it was affixed to the tree ; not only was Christ crucified, but the law came thereby to its end, as far as God's people were concerned. We are now placed under Christ. We are now regarded as being "in the Spirit," for Christ is our life and the Holy Ghost is the power of that life.

Well, here then he says that it was needful that he should exhort them to "earnestly contend for the faith which was once delivered to the saints." This is what is on my heart to speak about. How great is, not only "conversion" such as the O.T. people knew before faith came but, the "salvation" which is now, as the apostle Paul says in Ephesians (i. 13), "the word of truth, the gospel of your (not conversion but the gospel of your) salvation"! This is what was added consequent upon redemption. Nobody could have been delivered from hell without

being converted ; but the " gospel of our salvation "
is to make us perfectly happy on earth, to bring us
into cloudless peace and liberty while here in this
world. It is this that is new, from the cross of Christ.
Why, beloved friends, it is new to many children of
God now ! They are not sure at all, even those that
are most real ; with many it is only a " humble
hope." But through God's mercy, I take it for
granted that we have all learned this, more or less,
the more the better. I do say that this is an all-
important thing. Sometimes, when persons are
seeking to come into fellowship, there is an idea
of the importance of their understanding the church.
How they are to understand the church I do not
know. I did not understand it when I first began to
break bread. I never saw any that did. I have seen
persons that thought they did, and they had to
correct their thoughts afterwards. We should not
expect this knowledge. Possibly, of the saints in
communion who have been in fellowship for forty
years, there may be many who have not even yet
arrived at a true knowledge of what the church is.
But to ask it from a dear soul that has not long been
saved ! Ah, that is the point—not only " converted," but brought into liberty and peace. I do
say we ought to look for that before we get them to
the table of the Lord ; and we are not on proper
Christian ground till we know that we are saved.
This is what the gospel gives. It is not a hope of
being saved, but knowing it in a simple straight-

forward, intelligent, Christian manner. However, the word " intelligence " might leave room for our active brethren to find difficulties ! I do not want to put difficulties in the way of any, still less in the way of a soul that is trembling and uncertain.

The great requirement for souls seeking fellowship, and, I think, the only requirement, is that they should be settled firmly on Christ and Christ's salvation as a known present thing. Perhaps we find a person that cannot stand that. I recommend them to hear the gospel. There are plenty of saints who want to hear a full gospel. I do not say a free gospel. A full gospel does not convert many souls. A free gospel may do so. A free gospel may be used to awaken many, to cause exercise, but a full gospel will bring the answer to all these difficulties. Peter, I may say, preached a free gospel, and Paul a full one. Most of the children of God have not got a full gospel. It is essential that they should, before they can take their place as members of the body of Christ. Suppose they come in without it : perhaps the first hymn that is given out is an expression of thanksgiving that every question is settled for ever, and they are thus called to sing about themselves what they do not believe, and do not know about. They sing (in, what I call, a slipshod manner, without any conscience) what may not be true of their state, what is too much for them. Well, all that is a very unhappy state of things, and ought not to be. But if they are brought into the liberty of Christ,

before they are received, not expecting from them
clearness of intelligence, but knowing that their
souls are set free (and nothing less than that should
be looked for), then things go on happily. They
learn quite fast enough when they come in, provided they have liberty in their souls. The lack of it
is the barrier against learning. If I have difficulties
about my soul with God for ever, it is no good to tell
me about other things ; and, therefore, wherever
that is passed over lightly, there is a barrier. But
as to everything else, well, one thing at a time is
quite as much as we can bear, and people who grasp
everything at the same moment, I am afraid, grasp
nothing. All is apt to be cloudy in their minds, and
that is not " the faith that was once delivered to the
saints."

" The faith " is not a mere mist. Mysteries are
not mists or clouds. Mysteries are the firmest things
in the Bible. The N.T. is full of mysteries—mystery
" concerning Christ and the church," " the mystery
of God," " the mystery of the gospel," " the mystery
of the faith." Mystery means what was not revealed
in O.T. times ; now it is. That is just our privilege.
Even Christ Himself, in the way that we receive
Him now, is a mystery. Do we simply believe on
Him as the Messiah ? " Great is the mystery of
godliness ; God [or, He Who] was manifested in
flesh, was justified in Spirit, seen of angels, preached
among Gentiles, believed on in [the] world, received
up in glory " (1 Tim. iii. 16). This is Christ as we

know Him now. Everything is mystery in Christianity, even the way Christ is received. He was not known so before. It takes in the gospel, " the gospel of our salvation," the clear riddance from all hindrances. Is not the assembly a mystery ? Is it not a truth of the greatest moment for every member of the body of Christ to know ? And when you have your convert, when the soul is there brought to know the gospel, then show him what the church is, as best you can. Take trouble with him. Do not imagine he knows what he does not know. Where is he to learn if not inside ? He will never learn by staying away. The church of God is not only the great place of incomparable blessing and enjoyment, it is also the great school. Well, the soul wants to go to school. Will he find a better school outside ?

Even the best of those who are outside—that is, those that are not gathered to the name of the Lord, they are mostly occupied about salvation for themselves, or if not that, about work for others. What can you expect better ? They do not know the relationships into which they are brought. Take the question that is now so uppermost in people's minds—priesthood. What an Evangelical would say to meet priestly pretension is, that it is all a mistake to suppose that there are any priests but Christ. Is that where you are ? The truth that God has shown us is, that all Christians alike are priests. When you are only on Evangelical ground, it is not the assertion of positive possession of privilege, it is merely denying an error, a negative way of looking at things. Many would indeed admit that we are all priests, but they do not see how it is applied. If they are all priests unto God, they should be allowed to express their praise, and others join (Heb. x. 22) " Let us " (not you, he puts himself along with those to whom he was writing—let us) draw " near " into the holiest. Were this really applied, people might want to express their audible praises to God sometimes, and this would be considered disorderly. Do you think that we are always as careful as we ought to be ? There are two words of moment in the First Epistle to the Corinthians—the first is, " in order," the other is, " to edification." All things should be done " in order," and " to edification " (1 Cor. xiv. 26, 40). How are we to judge of what is done ? It is laid down in this very chapter. Why do we forget it sometimes ?

A question was put to me, whether it is according to scripture that, at what is called an assembly meeting, or other meeting of a similar character, more than two should speak. What is laid down as to this ? That two, or at most three, might speak (1 Cor. xiv. 27, 29). Where there are more, I should be disposed to get away as fast as possible. You are mistaken about your liberty. We have only liberty to do what the Lord says ; and I can see the wisdom of this limitation. There might be plenty of time for half a dozen speakers, but still the order is clear, " two, or at most three." There can be no question about the meaning. It certainly does not mean that there might not be half a dozen prayers by different people, but that formal speaking, even of prophets, had its limits. And surely the lesser gifts have not a greater liberty than the greater ones ! The prophets had the highest gift, and yet it is said, they were only to speak two or three. The plain meaning of it is that there never ought to be, under any excuse, more than two or three. Too much of a good thing is as bad as too little. If you have too much of what is even good, it is apt to make you sick : you must leave room for proper digestion. Hence the wisdom in the restriction as to numbers.

So it is—what seems to me to be so very plain— that we have not got merely the facts given and the commandment of the Lord, but good reason given. There is perfect wisdom, there is not such a thing as an arbitrary word in all the Bible. All the rules and regulations, commandments and precepts, are pregnant with divine wisdom.

It is a long while since " brethren " first began ; but there never was a time when we are more called to see whether we are really " contending earnestly for the faith once for all (not " once on a time," but, " once for all ") delivered to the saints." May God forbid that we should ever swerve in the least degree ! We are not competent to say what a little beginning of divergence may lead to. It might be apparently a little beginning, but alas, a little beginning of a great evil.

The Lord give us simple fidelity, and in all love to
our brethren. I never think of my brethren being
merely such as are gathered to the name of the
Lord Jesus ; and I feel most deeply the undermining that is going on everywhere of things that
were once undisputed.

VERSE 3

JUDE, then, was in full expectation of a departure
from " the faith," and that it would be necessary to
defend the faith. He evidently had had it on his
heart to speak to them of comforting things, things
that are always bright and sweet to the believer ;
but the circumstances called for alarm, for solemn
warning. This is never very acceptable to people.
They prefer things smooth ; but the apostle himself,
or the writer, whether an apostle or not—the writer's
whole heart would have delighted in dwelling on all
that was comforting and strengthening to the
soul. But, my brethren, what is the good of that if
the foundations are being undermined ? This is
what you must look at. Therefore he draws attention
to the fact that the faith was " once for all delivered."
" Once " is an equivocal word. It might mean " once
on a time," once at a particular moment ; but this
is not the force of the word here at all. It means
" once for all." And what a blessing it is that we
have in this book (and more particularly in the
books of the New Testament), the holy deposit

which we are called upon to believe, given us in full, "once for all." There is not a truth to be received that is not revealed in the word of God. There is not a difficulty nor a departure from the truth which is not in one way or another there guarded against. We, therefore, never require to go outside the revelation of God ; and this explains why God permitted, in the early apostolic days, that there should be a deal of evil. Does it surprise us that there should have been gross disorders among the Corinthians, for instance, even at the table of the Lord ? Well, one is naturally struck at first sight by such a fact. How was it that when there was such power of the Holy Ghost, that when there were miracles wrought, that when there were prophets prophesying (the highest form of teaching), that at the same time and place, the saints that gathered on the Lord's Day, broke out into a disorder that we never find even in the present day, or very rarely ? How could God more guard *us* than by allowing it then ? It is always a very delicate matter to deal with evil, either of doctrine, or practice, or service, or government, or worship, or anything that you can speak of. It was of the very greatest moment, there-fore, that God, in view of the evils that would, some time or another, appear in the church, should allow the germ of the evils to appear then ; and, for this reason, that we might have divinely given directions for dealing with the evils when they did appear. Consequently, we are not taking the place of setting

up to legislate ; but we are not at liberty to depart
from the word. This has been given us by the Holy
Ghost. We are called to find therein everything that
becomes us as saints, and for every part of our work
to find a principle, and example too, sufficient to
guide us ; so that we may never set up any will of
our own about a matter, and that we may always
find God expressing, in one form or another, His
will. What we have to do is to seek to learn from
Him, and to apply the result, either to ourselves for
our own correction, or to other people for their
warning.

Now that is the reason why there is such great
moment in Jude's calling to mind that the faith was
" once," and " once for all," delivered to the
saints. And, as a point of fact, I do not think we
shall ever find in scripture such a thing as a mere
repetition. Sometimes you may have scriptures
that approach very closely, and in the New Testament you could hardly have it more than in these
two Epistles of Peter and Jude. But I am about
to point out to you, what will appear as I go along
still more completely, that, while there are resemblances between these two writers, who are both
speaking of the terrible evil that was about to flood
the church ; and who naturally approach each
other, yet there is a marked difference between them.
It is always the difference that is the special lesson
for us to learn. Where the two approach, it confirms.
We can say, " In the mouth of two or three witnesses

shall every word be established." But where there is a divergence, and a distinction is to be seen in the lessons that they convey, we have evidently more than we might have had if we had only had one of the writers. The same thing is true, not merely in these two Epistles, but in Ephesians and Colossians for example. The resemblance there is so great that a favourite theory of the Rationalists is that the Epistle to the Colossians is the only one that Paul ever wrote, and that the one to the Ephesians is only an enlarged and inflated copy (written, perhaps, by a contemporary of the apostle) ; and, accordingly, that the latter has not the same divine (though I ought not, perhaps, to use that word) value—that it has not Paul's value. These men do not believe in divine value, they do not believe in God having written these Epistles ; but some of them do believe that Paul wrote that to the Colossians, but deny his having written the one to the Ephesians. A very learned man, who translated all the Bible (and, indeed, his is one of the best of the German translations), is one of this school. So that you may learn from this, that there are persons who have laboured all through their lives on the Bible, who nevertheless did not believe the Bible—*i.e.*, really and truly. He, of course, would have entirely objected to such an account being given of him. But what matters what people object to, if it is true ! He was a leading man in his day, and I hope that he was not without looking to Christ before his decease. But at any rate, what

he did during his life was a sad departure from the
truth of God, from " the faith that was once for all
delivered to the saints."

Having then already dwelt a little upon what is
one important and primary element of " the faith,"
I add, further, that believers are brought into great
relationships. Not only are we " converted " and
" saved," being brought into peace and liberty, but
we are called to realise also that we are no longer
merely English persons or French, Jews or Gentiles,
but that we are children of God, and that we are
such now. We, therefore, turn our backs on our
boasting in our nation and our city, and our family,
and all these various forms of men's vanity, which is
merely boasting of something of the flesh. We are
called out of that now. This is also part of " the
faith once delivered." In Christ there is neither Jew
nor Gentile, bond nor free (Gal. iii. 28). What does
this mean ? It means just what I have been saying.

Well then, again, we are made members of Christ's
body ; and this is a relationship which so many of
God's children are so slow to believe. They think
and talk of their being members of the Wesleyan
body, or Presbyterian body, or Baptist, of this body,
or that body, no matter what it is. Well, they say,
to be sure we are members of Christ's body, too !
Yes, but if people valued the truth of their member-
ship of Christ's body, what would the other be in
their eyes ? Simply nothing at all. Where do you
find the Presbyterian body, or the Episcopal body,

or the Congregational body in the N.T.? Where do
you find the Baptist body in the N.T.? There was an
approach to this party spirit in the very earliest
days—" I am of Paul, I am of Apollos, I am of
Cephas " (1 Cor. i. 12). Well, there you have the
germ of it. And these germs never perish. It is
not only that blessed germs of truth do not perish
and are meant to take root and bear fruit, and
consequently they are perpetuated here and there ;
but alas, evil germs do the same. And what is more,
another thing is not a germ exactly, but is a leaven—
a corrupt and a corrupting thing that is very pala-
table, making the wheaten bread to be lighter to the
taste and pleasanter for some palates to partake of.
And, at any rate, this leaven, whatever may be the
case with the bread, is the corrupting influence
at work among the saints in two forms. In Corinth
it was the corruption of morals ; in Galatia it was the
corruption of doctrine. There you have it at work.
When our Lord was here He confronted the same
thing in the Pharisees and Sadducees. The Sadducees
were the great corruptors morally ; the Pharisees
were the great religionists, or rather were strong for
doctrine.   But the Sadducees were sapping all
doctrines by denying the truth. There you have the
two things again—doctrinal leaven and corrupting
leaven ; at any rate there was " the leaven of the
Pharisees and Sadducees," however you may des-
cribe it. There were also the Herodians—a worldly
leaven, a pandering to the Roman court, not merely

accepting the Romans as having power and authority
from God, but trying to please them in order to make
their own position better and their circumstances
easier. So that you see what a very weighty truth
is this, calling for earnest examination, to take care
that we do not infringe upon or weaken our certainty
in that faith which was "once delivered to the
saints." Are we indifferent about it ? Have we an
interest in it ? Have we only partially received it,
and are we content with that ? Or are we resolved
by the grace of God to refuse everything that is not
the faith that was once for all delivered ? Are we
resolved to receive and maintain that faith in all its
integrity ? That is what we are called to do.

VERSES 4, 5

Now this attitude was the more important ; " for,"
as he says, " certain men have crept in unawares."
Jude is not quite so advanced, in point of time, as
John. When John wrote his First Epistle, the bad
people went out—the antichrists went out (1 John
ii. 19). But the danger here was that they were
within. Certain men had crept in, as it were, unawares. That is, they had fair appearances at first,
of course. " They, who before of old were ordained
to this sentence " (" condemnation " is not exactly
the meaning of the word—" to this judgment ")
" ungodly men turning the grace of our God into

lasciviousness and denying our only Master* and Lord Jesus Christ " (ver. 4).

This, you see, is the prominent thing in Jude's mind : so that, under fair appearances, they were undermining moral principles, they were turning the grace of God into lasciviousness. This was the worst evil, as far as morals were concerned, that Jude warns them against in this Epistle ; but then this evil is connected with a doctrinal error. They denied two things. In Peter they denied only one. There they denied the Sovereign Master that bought them (2 Pet. ii. 1). Peter does not say that they were redeemed. It is a great mistake to confound being " bought " with being " redeemed." All the world is bought, but only believers are redeemed. Universal purchase is a truth of God ; universal redemption is a falsehood. Redemption implies that we have the forgiveness of sins. You see that clearly in the Epistles. Take, for instance, that to the Ephesians, " In Whom we have redemption through His blood, the forgiveness of trespasses, according to the riches of His grace " (i. 7). Now it is clear that the great mass of mankind have not redemption through His blood ; but they are all bought, and the believer is bought too, and we are constantly exhorted on the ground, not only of our being redeemed, but of our being bought. For instance, the Corinthians are told that they were bought. That is the reason why

* Θεόν (God) though added (after "Master ") by KLP 31 Syrr., is omitted by ℵABC 13 Vulg. Copt. Sah. Arm. and Æthiopic Versions.

they should not act as if they were their own masters.
We have not any rights of our own (1 Cor. vi.).
We are not at liberty to say, I think it quite right
to go to a Court of Law in order to maintain my
rights. No, I am bound, if I am summoned as a
witness, to go ; I am bound, if people go to law with
me, to go. But on the contrary, to insist on my own
rights ! why do not I rather suffer wrong ? That is
the way the apostle Paul looks at it. And who is
the apostle ? The voice of God, the commandments
of the Lord.

So that you see I come at once to the question of
the faith, if really I believe what I may talk very
glibly about as if I did. The difficulty is to find faith
on the earth. As the Lord has said, " When the Son
of man cometh, shall He find faith on the earth ? "
Evidently, therefore, this departure from the faith
is supposed by that very question of our Lord Jesus.
Only here, the solemn thing is, that it is pressed on
those who once bore the name of the Lord. They
may go on for a while, for years ; and there may be
only some little things that one feels here or there,
or their departure may not take anything like so
terrible a form as here, but the question is, Where
will it end ? When once we get on the incline of our
own rights, our own will ; when once we abandon
His Sovereignty, and, more than that, that He is
not only Sovereign Master but our Lord ; who can
say what may not ensue ?

Now here we get a closer relationship. Peter, in

his Epistle, only supposes that universal place of our Lord. Why does Jude add, " denying our . . . Lord Jesus Christ " ? Because he looks at that special following of those that are called by His name—on whom the name of the Lord is called. Here, therefore, we find a subtler and a deeper denial than the denial of the Sovereign Master in Peter. That of course was very far outside and very gross—" sects of perdition, and denying the Sovereign Master that bought them." But here, in Jude, it is not only denying the Sovereign Master of the world, of everything ; but " our Lord," the One to Whom we belong, the One to Whose name we are baptised, the One Whom we profess to value and acknowledge to be our life and righteousness, and our all—denying Him !

You must not imagine that these things all come out in a short time. There is a little beginning of departure ; but when your back is turned to the Lord and you follow that path, where will it end ? No man can tell ; but the Spirit of God can and does, and He shows that these little departures end in a fearful ditch of the enemy ; and so He says :

" But I would remind you, though once for all knowing all things*, that [the] Lord having saved a people out of Egypt's land, in the second place destroyed those that believed not " (ver. 5). Here we have again the same word " once," which as we

---

* πάντα (all things) ℵABC² 13 Vulg. Copt. Syr. Arm. and Æthiop. Vv. instead of τοῦτο (this) KL 31 and Sah. Version.

have already seen is equivocal. It might mean
formerly ; but that is not the meaning at all, no
more than that the faith was formerly given. It
means given " once for all."

Well, he says, " once for all knowing," not only
" this," but " all about it." The word " this " is now
in critical texts changed into " all things," and this is
exactly the position of the believer, which is the
reason why we are so very responsible. Do you
recollect what the apostle John says to the " babes "
of the family ? " Ye have an unction from the Holy
One, and ye know all things " (1 John ii. 20). How
did that come to pass ? We are not in the habit of
regarding babes so wise as this ; yet what the apostle
says must be true. The only question is—In what
sense did he mean that they knew all things ? I
think the meaning is this. The babe has got Christ
just as much as an apostle. Having Christ, he has the
truth—all the truth. There it is ; and he has also
got the Holy Ghost—an unction from the Holy
One. Therefore, he has got power in the gift of the
Holy Ghost ; for a babe has this gift. It is not the
privilege only of the advanced learners in the school
of Christ. The babes of the family of God have got
Christ perfectly. They may draw it out very im-
perfectly. They may be able to look upon Christ,
and speak of Christ in very hesitating terms as far
as their intelligence goes, but such is their place and
their privilege. Accordingly, Jude presses here
their privilege of " once for all knowing all things."

Where were they now ? They were in great danger.
You often see this in the early beginnings of saints.
They are very bright at first ; they are not easily
stumbled by anything they hear from the Bible ;
they receive it with simplicity, and delight in it.
They, then, are knowing all things, in the sense in
which the apostle speaks here. It is not a question
of intelligence, but of simplicity and of a single eye,
and when the eye is single the whole body is full of
light. Thus they had it by the power of the Spirit of
God, and it was not at all a question of their being
great adepts in controversy, or showing a wonderful
knowledge of the types, or anything of that kind.
I call that intelligence. But this is the singleness of
eye that looks to Christ and sees the truth in Christ,
and is not troubled by the difficulties that people are
always apt to feel when they begin to reason, when
love gets cold and they have questions of duty.
Then they cannot see clearly ; then a trial is made on
their faith to which it is not equal ; then they begin
to get dark, as well as to doubt. This is just where
these saints appear to me to have been, whom the
writer is here addressing as " once knowing all
things." They knew not only the faith, but these
terrible things that are coming in.

However, Jude recalls them to their remembrance :
" I will therefore put you in remembrance, though
once for all knowing all things, how that [the]
Lord, having saved a people out of [the] land of
Egypt, afterward destroyed them that believed not."

That fact is a very solemn thing for the writer to
bring before them ; and it was meant to solemnize
them, to deliver them from that careless state of
soul which takes for granted that, because we have
all been so blessed and led into the truth, no harm
can happen. Why, on the contrary, beloved friends,
for whom do you think Satan has the greatest
hatred out of all on the face of the earth ? Why,
any that are following the Lord with simplicity ;
any that are truly devoted to the Lord. His great
object is to try and stumble such, to turn them aside,
to bring difficulties into their minds and make them
hesitate. Now, where souls are simple and single-
eyed, they have not these difficulties at all ; but
when they do not go on cleaving to the Lord with
full purpose of heart, they begin to forget what they
once knew. It is no longer Christ applied to judge
everything here ; they allow their own thoughts,
their own feelings, their own mind, their own conceit,
perhaps to lead them ; but, whatever it is, it is not
Christ, and now He brings this fact before them.
Why, look at the history that you have in the very
beginning of the Old Testament. God had a people
once before us, and, what is more, God saved that
people. That is the very thing—He did save them.
It was not only that He passed over them in the land
of Egypt, but there was His mighty arm at the Red
Sea that crushed their enemies and saved themselves,
and brought them into the desert that He might
teach them what was in their heart, and let them

know what was in His. But they went back to
Egypt in their heart, and they could see no blessed-
ness in Canaan, the heavenly land to which the Lord
was leading them on—to Canaan, type of heaven,
the land of God's delight and glory ; they could see
nothing in it, and they did see that in the desert there
were serpents sometimes to bite those that refused
to learn from God ; and, further, that the Lord, if
He hearkened to their lusting after flesh, made the
flesh to come out of them as it were through their
nostrils, as a judgment upon their not being satisfied
with the manna, the bread of heaven. All these
things happened, and what was the result ? All
perished in the wilderness excepting two men :
Caleb and Joshua.

Now Jude says, That is your danger. You must
remember that you cannot tell for certain whether
a person has life eternal. Every man ought to know
that for himself ; every woman ought to know that
for herself. If a person believes that he or she has
life eternal in Christ, they are called to follow the
Lord with full purpose of heart. And if they do not
follow Him so, or if attracted by anything worldly,
or by pursuits of their own from day to day, they
neglect the Lord and His word, and neglect prayer
and all the helps that the Lord gives us, which we so
deeply need for our souls—what will be the end of
that ? Just what Jude is showing them here : " I
will therefore put you in remembrance, though ye
once knew all things, how that the Lord having

saved a people out of the land of Egypt, afterwards destroyed them that believed not."

It turned out that they were not true believers, after all. The same thing applies now : " These things happened unto them for types ; and they are written for our admonition."

VERSES 6–8

" AND angels which kept not their own original estate, but abandoned their proper dwelling, He hath kept in everlasting bonds under gloom unto [the] great day's judgment ; as Sodom and Gomorrah and the cities around them, having in the like manner with them greedily committed fornication and gone after strange flesh, lie there an example, undergoing judgment of eternal fire. Yet likewise, these dreamers also defile flesh, and set at nought lordship and rail at dignities " (vers. 6–8.)

If we compare this chapter of Jude with the Second Epistle of Peter, we get a very clear view of the precise difference between the two. No doubt there is a great deal that is common in both Epistles ; but it is the difference that is of great account in taking a view of scripture, as has been already observed. In these two Epistles there may be many points in common, but the two accounts are thoroughly different. The same thing is true as regards all the testimony that God gives us. The marks of difference are the great criteria.

You will notice that Peter, after alluding to false teachers, alludes to " sects of perdition " (2 Pet. ii. 1). The word heterodoxy gives a different idea. There was something of this difference in the minds of the apostles that ought to be in ours, viz . :—a very strong horror of the breach amongst those who belong to Christ and the church that He formed in unity here. There is a certain wilfulness that is particularly offensive to God. People now have so little sense of " wrongness " that they think it a natural thing that people should be justified in doing what they like ; but to look at the matter in that sense would be to give up God. Perhaps men can be trusted in matters of ordinary life to form a sufficiently sound judgment as regards certain things, such as being careful of their food and careful of their dress, and also as regards other things that belong to this life. We find that God says little on the matter, except to guard His children from the vanity of the world and the pride of life. Still there is nothing technical or narrow laid down in the word of God. But it is quite another thing, when we consider that Christ died to " gather together into one the children of God that were scattered abroad " (John xi. 52), that we should allow ourselves to extenuate a wilful departure from the right course, by allowing our own notions to carry us away therefrom. Persons should not allow themselves to do this kind of thing, nor should they think that they are superior to others, which is generally a

great delusion on their part. You will not find that
men who are devoted to Christ set themselves up in
this way, because we all know that Christ teaches
us to count others better than ourselves. That may
become merely a foolish sentiment by the separating
us from a spirit of power and of love, and of a sound
mind. We are to judge of everything by Christ. If
we let in " self," we are sure to go wrong. This
readiness to see Christ in everything is a happy
thing when it is applied to our dealings with our
brothers and sisters. It is not that others *are*
necessarily better than ourselves, it is that we are
to count them so in our spirit and in our dealings
with them. When Christ is before us, we can afford
to judge our sins as stronger than those of others.
We are well aware of our faults ; but it is only
when we are much occupied with others' doings
that we know much about their faults. The great
thing is that we are to see Christ as our guide, and
we are to judge ourselves in ourselves ; we are also
to see Christ in others and to love them, and to
count them better than ourselves.

There are other senses in which people get into
this spirit of sect, and thereby give an improper
value to certain views. For instance, with regard to
baptism. In modern times, at any rate, and very
likely also in ancient times, there is, I suppose,
hardly anything that has troubled the church more
than this subject. By some people, a superstitious
value is given to baptism, causing them, as it were,

to despise those who have a reasoning turn of mind,
and those who have a strong theory and notions
about the Jewish remnant ; but, so far as I know, the
Jewish remnant has nothing to do with Christian
baptism, because the handing it over to the Jewish
remnant means giving up *our* relation to Christ.
For Christian people, who are already walking in
the ways of the Lord, to be occupied with baptism
is, in my opinion, a most extraordinary inversion
of all that is wise and right, because Christian people
have passed through that experience already. Perhaps, when the ceremony was performed it was not
done in the best way, and we may think that, therefore, if we had known then what we know now we
might have been more careful in its performance.
Baptism is merely an external visible confession of
the Lord Jesus, and for persons who have been
confessing the Lord for twenty, thirty, or forty
years, to be occupied with baptism seems to me to
be an extraordinary change from all that is wise.
Baptism is an initiatory step ; our Christianity
begins when we begin our Christian confession—we
should, therefore, be going forward, not backward.

Baptism has even been used as the badge of a
sect, and time would fail to narrate the many other
ways in this regard. But here, in Peter's Epistle,
we have a darker thing referred to—" sects of
perdition " (2 Pet. ii. 1). It evidently was not merely
a sect, but a sect of perdition. In this case, the sect
of perdition was evidently something very dreadful,

and it was apparently against the Lord, because the words are " denying the Sovereign Master that bought them." This, as we have already remarked, is not " redemption " but " purchase," and so takes in all men whether converted or not. It is the denial of His rights over all as the Sovereign Master. So, too, Peter begins at once with the flood, the deluge, but there is not a word about that in Jude. This is another great mark of difference to note, the manner in which the denial of the Lord is described, and how we find God's mode of dealing with this matter. So one sees the propriety of the flood being brought in by Peter, because it was the universal unrightcousness and rebelliousness of the whole world. Jude, on the other hand, was not given to look at that particularly, but at the hostility that is shown to the truth and to Christ. Peter looks at the general unrighteousness of mankind, and so he says : " For if God spared not angels when they sinned, but cast them down to lowest hell and delivered them up to chains of gloom reserved for judgment, and spared not an ancient world, but preserved Noah, an eighth [person], a preacher of righteousness, having brought a flood upon a world of ungodly ones ; and reducing to ashes [the] cities of Sodom and Gomorrah, He condemned [them] with an overthrow, having set an example to those that should live ungodily ;   and rescued just Lot " etc. (2 Pet. ii. 4–7).

What makes the reference again more remarkable

is that Jude speaks of the " angels that kept not
their own estate," but Peter of " angels that sinned,"
and who consequently come under the dealing of
God. The flood is upon the world of the ungodly,
and the cities of Sodom and Gomorrah are turned
into ashes for an example to those that should live
ungodily ; but just Lot was delivered because
he was a just man. The want of righteousness
brought this punishment upon everyone. It is
their general ungodliness, but no doubt there is a
particularity which Jude takes up, whilst Peter
takes up the universality. This is the marked
difference between the two. I have dwelt upon this
because it shows what the world of modern unbelief
is—what is called higher criticism. For these men
have been struck by the resemblance between this
Epistle of Jude and the Second Epistle of Peter ;
but with all their boasting of unbelief they have not
got the discernment to see that there is a marked
difference between the two. These men have been
caught by the superficial resemblance of the two
Epistles ; but when you, as it were, lift up the
superficial veil in which these Epistles agree, you
will find that the colours are different. You will
find darker colours in Jude than in Peter, although
it is bad enough in Peter, most terribly evil. But it
is of a general kind ; whereas, Jude was led by the
Holy Ghost to devote himself to the peculiar form
that wickedness takes when it turns from the grace
of God, when it turns to licentiousness.

Hence Jude begins with what is not referred to in
Peter at all, and it is for this reason that I read verse
5 over a second time to-night. " I will, therefore,
put you in remembrance, though once for all
knowing all things, that the Lord, having saved a
people "—mark that—" out of the land of Egypt "—
that is the sovereign grace that shows the salvation.
I am not speaking of it now as eternal salvation. It
was sovereign grace that chose Israel ; they were
not chosen for everlasting glory, but only delivered
out of Egypt. That surely shows a manifestation of
God's goodness, Who, instead of allowing them to
be oppressed and terrorised over by the cruel
Egyptians, smote the Egyptians and delivered His
people. They came into the narrower circle in one
sense of what were God's people, in one sense also
they were saved ; but they gave up the grace, they
abandoned God. This latter is what Jude has
particularly in view. He looks at Christendom as
being about to abandon the truth. He shows that
whatever the special favour shown by God, men will
get away from and deny it ; and further, that instead
of using grace to walk morally, they will take
advantage of grace to allow of a kind of immorality—
they will turn the grace of God into licentiousness.

Peter says nothing about this, but Jude does ;
so that it is evident that these learned men (who
think they are so clever in showing that Jude and
Peter are merely imitators of one another, and that
it is the same thing in substance in both—that there

is no particular difference, that they are in fact the same human picture), do not see God in either. Now, what we are entitled to is to see God in both Epistles, and what is more we should hear God's voice in both. You see then that Jude begins with this solemn fact that the Lord " having saved a people out of the land of Egypt "—I am giving now the strict force of the word—" the second time " (that He acted) " destroyed those that believed not." The first act was that He " saved " them, He brought them out by means of the paschal lamb, which was His first great act of " saving." The first time that God's glory appeared and He put Himself at the head of His people, He saved them out of the land of Egypt. What was " the second time " ? When He " destroyed " them. It is not vague, but it specifically mentions " the second time " ; this is the great point. At the time the golden calf was set up, that was the beginning of " the second time," and God went on smiting and smiting until everyone was destroyed except Caleb and Joshua. That was the second time. This went on for forty years, but it is all brought together in the words " the second time." God " destroyed them that believed not." That is the charge brought against them. Their carcases were falling in the wilderness. In Hebrews iii. (as is very evident also in the book of Numbers and elsewhere) there is this threat during their passage through the wilderness. It is one of the great facts of the books of Moses. As regards those

that came out of Egypt, they came under the hand
of God; some perished at one time, some at another,
but all perished in one way or the other, until all
disappeared ; and yet they had all been " saved "
out of the land of Egypt by the Lord.

Oh, what a solemn thing to set this before us now !
When I say before us, I mean before the church of
God, before all that bear the name of the Lord Jesus
here below. This is put expressly as a sample of the
solemn ways of God to be recollected in Christendom.
Then Jude also refers to the angels. I think the
wisdom of that is evident. Peter begins with the
angels and then goes on to refer to the flood. I
think, therefore, if any person looks at Genesis vi.
he will find a great deal of wisdom in Jude's reference.
I am well aware, of course, that there are many
that view " the sons of God " in a very different way
to what it appears to me. They are sometimes
very surprised, and expect one to be able to answer
all their questions. I do not assume any such com-
petency. I admire the wisdom of God in that God
does not stop to explain. He feels the awful iniquity
of what occurred in reference to these angels. They
are fallen angels, and of quite a different class to
those who fell before Adam was tempted.

It appears there were at least two falls of angels ;
one was he whom we call Satan—when man was
made, Satan tempted man through Eve. Those
ordinary evil angels, of which we read in the Bible
from Genesis down to Revelation, are not under ever-

lasting chains at all. They are roving about the
world continually, and so far from being in chains of
darkness, in "tortures" as it is called here, they
are allowed access to heaven. You will see that in a
very marvellous way in the history of Job. A great
many believers do not believe in the book of Job.
You will see there "the sons of God" referred to.
What is meant by "the sons of God" there? Why,
the angels of God. The angels of God appeared before
God. We learn from this that they have access, and
include not only the good angels but also the Satanic
angels. Satan was a fallen angel, but still he was an
angel, and when "the sons of God" came, Satan
was there too. So that it is evident, from the Book
of Revelation more particularly, that Satan will
not lose that access to the presence of God until we
are actually in heaven. It has not come to pass yet.
People have an extraordinary idea in their heads
that whatever access Satan had before that time,
he lost it—either when our Lord was born, or when
our Lord died—but there is nothing of this in the
Epistle to the Ephesians, where, on the contrary,
it is expressly stated that our wrestling is not against
flesh and blood, but against wicked spirits in the
heavenlies. We are not like the Israelites fighting
against Canaanites. Our Canaanite is a spiritual
enemy in heavenly places, that is, Satan and his host
of demons or angels.

But, as we have seen, these are not at all the sins
that are referred to here. There is a marked differ-

ence. There is a character of iniquity that these
angels fell into on earth, and so a distinct difference
in their doom. These angels fell into a very peculiar
iniquity, which is in a general way spoken of in
Peter, but in a special way in Jude. They were put
under chains of darkness and not allowed to stir out
of their prison. They are not the angels that tempt
us now. They did their bad work just a little time
before the flood. That fact gives the matter a very
solemn character. If people want to know how it
was done, that I do not know ; but you are called
upon to believe, just as much as I am. What
Genesis vi. does say is that there were " sons of God "
upon earth at that time who acted in a way contrary to everything in relation to God, and which
was so offensive to Him that He would not allow
the earth to go on any longer, and this is what
brought on the flood. No doubt too there was also
a general iniquity in mankind that brought the
flood upon them. Man was very corrupt and man
was vile, but besides that there was this awful
violation of the marks that divide the creatures of
God in some mysterious manner. Hence God completely destroyed the whole framework of creation,
and put an end to them and their offspring, so that
every one of them perished. That is what took place
then. Of course, you will tell me that they could not
perish absolutely. No, I admit that these angels
could not perish any more than men such as you ;
but this is what God did with those angels that

behaved in that tremendously wicked manner. They
became prisoners, they were put under confinement,
not like Satan and his host that tempt us to this
day, but these particular angels were not allowed to
tempt men any more. They had done too much,
and God would not allow these things to go on any
longer, therefore there was this mighty interference
at the time of the flood, and not only the things that
generally inflict men. These are the words, " Angels
that kept not their first estate." Their falling was a
departure from their first estate. In this very case
Satan had not done so, nor had the angels that fell
with Satan. But it was quite another kind of
iniquity that caused the flood. These angels left
their own habitation and preferred to take their
place among mankind to act as if they were men on
earth, and accordingly, God has now reserved them
in everlasting chains under darkness until the
judgment of the great day. Nobody can say that
this is true of Satan and his host, but if people
should think this, I do not see how they can read
these verses and give such a meaning to them. Satan
will be cast into the bottomless pit for a thousand
years, but their years do not run out until the
judgment of the great day comes. Then they will be
judged everlastingly.

What makes the matter so striking is that Jude
compares this conduct, and this awful opposition to
all the landmarks that divide angels from mankind,
with Sodom and Gomorrah. We know that the

enormity of this wickedness exceeded that even of all wicked people. So here their sin brings them into juxtaposition with Sodom and Gomorrah, " Even as Sodom and Gomorrah and the cities about them in like manner to these, giving themselves over to fornication and going after strange flesh, are set forth for an example, suffering vengeance of eternal fire " (ver. 7).

When we come back to Peter and see what he has to say on this matter, it is, " For if God spared not the angels that sinned." Peter does not go further than that. Of course we know how they sinned— that is what Jude looks into. But here in Peter it is general " angels that sinned." He cast them down into hell and darkness, but that description does not apply to Satan and his host. Therefore it seems there were two different falls of angels ; one, Satan and his followers mounting up in the pride of their hearts to God, the other, these angels sinking down in the wickedness of their heart to man, to man in a very low condition indeed. The difference therefore is most marked. God " delivered them unto chains of darkness to be reserved to judgment, and spared not the old world." There is a connection between the two narratives, as it is about the same time. Peter marks this very point, and puts it along with God's dealing with the angels. This however is entirely left out by Jude. Peter says, " And spared not the old world, but saved Noah, the eighth [person]."

How is Noah described ?   As " a preacher of righteousness." Noah was not a preacher of grace. The grand truth that Noah proclaimed was that God was going to destroy the world by the deluge. That was exactly the right message. I do not think we are entitled to say he said nothing more, but the characteristic of Noah was that he was " a preacher of righteousness." This is precisely what occurs in Peter ; he does not bring out the grace of God at all, in his chapter. He is thundering at unrighteousness. He is giving with that trumpet of righteousness a very clear sound indeed. He is evidently giving out, in very dark and solemn words, the destruction that shall await the wicked at the great change ; and he shows that the same thing has happened before, and he begins, as far as man is concerned, not with Israel saved out of Egypt by God, but looks at the whole world destroyed. He is looking at the universality of unrighteousness, and not at the gradual departure of the people that were saved, saved first and lost afterwards. " He saved Noah, bringing in the flood upon the world of the ungodly." Peter then looks at the cities of the plain—more particularly Sodom and Gomorrah. He does not say anything about the special iniquity, but looks at it in a general way. " And turning the cities of Sodom and Gomorrah into ashes, condemned [them] with an overthrow, making [them] an ensample unto those that after should live ungodlily; and delivered just Lot vexed with the filthy conversation of the wicked. For that righteous man dwelling among them, in seeing and hearing, vexed his righteous soul from day to day with their unlawful deeds " (2 Pet. ii. 4–8).

So that instead of these two Epistles being alike, one of them a mere replica of the other, and an imitation in a clumsy way, they are both marked by most peculiarly different characteristics. And this is what deludes some men with all their criticism, and all the doctrine of the working of mind and the reasoning of rationalism is entirely outside the mark. Man's mind sees certain things in a general outside way and reasons upon it, flattering himself that he is doing something wonderful, and that he is bringing light when he is only spreading mist over the precious word of God, nothing but mist and darkness. So that the general difference between the two Epistles is very marked indeed.

Well then, we come now to the bearing of Peter's words upon the present time. " The Lord knoweth how to deliver the godly out of temptations, and to reserve the unjust unto the day of judgment to be punished." That is the practical testimony coming out of it. " But chiefly them that walk after the flesh in the lust of uncleanness, and despise government." It is not, you observe, simply corruptness. No, it is the larger view that is looked at. What would apply to Mahommedanism would apply to Judaism, would apply to heathenism, and would also apply to Christendom. The analogy is, that this particular form of evil requires a particular form of discipline, and that the world will be destroyed not by water but by fire from God in heaven. That is what I think is referred to by the " overthrow," and the reason of it ; " whereas angels, which are greater in power and might, bring not railing accusation against them before the Lord " (2 Pet. ii. 9–11).

But when we come to Jude, it is a great deal closer than all this. What he says is, " Likewise also these dreamers." I do not know any reason for putting in the word " filthy." You will see the word is in italics. There is a great deal of wickedness where there is nothing wrong in word. It is only in the idea, there may be nothing offensive, yet it is sapping and undermining all that is precious in those people who live in the imagination of their own hearts instead of being guided by the word of God. Why ? Because the word of God is an expression of God's authority, and His will is the only thing that ought to guide us, as well as all mankind. If that is true of man because he is the creature of God, how much more is it true of those whom He has begotten by the word of truth ! These latter are therefore called more particularly to heed and learn the word of God. I do not know anything of more practical importance than that. If I were to give, in one word, in what all practical Christianity consists, I should say—obedience ; and that obedience is entirely one of faith, not law. It is characterised in quite another way by Peter, " obedience of Jesus Christ," (1 Pet. i. 2) not obedience of Adam. Adam's obedience was that he was not to touch that particular tree, but now that God has revealed His will we are bound by that revealed will. To him that knoweth to do good and doeth it not, to him it is sin. It is not merely you must not do anything wrong in all those ways of men which show how far their heart is from God, but " to him that knoweth to do good and doeth it not, to him it is sin." Talk about James being legal ! obedience is his peculiar grace. He is the very one that speaks about " the law of liberty." The law of Moses was the law of bondage ; it was purposely to convict man of sin which he had in his nature, to crush all self-righteousness out of him. Whereas what James speaks of is the exercise of a new life that God's grace gives us, and of the love that Christ has revealed that we should be after the pattern of Christ. What was the difference between Christ's obedience and the Israelite's obedience ? The Israelite's was, Thou shalt not do this or that. But this is not what Christ says. Of course, Christ never did anything that was wrong. Christ was pleasing to God in every act of His life, in every feeling of His soul, in all that constituted walking with God here below. This is exactly what we are called here to do. This is what Peter means when he says, " Elect according to foreknowledge of God the Father through sanctification (or, in virtue of sanctification) of the Spirit unto obedience, and sprinkling of the blood, of Jesus Christ " (1 Pet. i. 1, 2).

The sprinkling is the sprinkling of the blood of

Jesus, and the reference is to Exodus xxiv., where Moses takes the book of the law and sprinkles it with blood, and he sprinkles the people too with blood ; everything being thus brought under death. It was the great mark of death having its sway. The book and the people were sprinkled with the blood shed, meaning death to any who failed to obey that book. Now the Christian in a way stands totally contrasted with that ; when he is converted his first desire is to do the will of God. When Saul of Tarsus was smitten down, his first words as a converted man were, " Lord, what wilt Thou have me to do ? " And this is what occurs even before we get peace. It is so with every converted person. His first desire is to do the will of God. He very little knows himself. He does not know how weak he is. He has got a bad nature counteracting him, but he has yet to learn the operation of the new nature that is in him. How does that new nature come ? By receiving the word of revealed grace. I do not say the work of Christ the Saviour, because Saul knew very well that he knew nothing ; but mercy and goodness struck him down and gave him a new nature that he once railed at. Paul knew Christ was saving him, but he did not know that we have to learn, not only the word of God, but the experimental way of finding our need of it. It is not only the Saviour that we want, but the mighty work that abolishes all our sins, and brings us to God in perfect peace and liberty through the redemption of the Lord Jesus.

It is not only that I am born again ; that I am going
to be saved by and by, but saved now. This is the
proper meaning of the Christian dispensation that
produces this desire even before I know that the
blood of Christ is screening me entirely. I want to
obey as Christ obeyed, not merely to do something
like the Jew, but I am doing it now because this
nature in me impels me to do it. It is the instinct
of the new man. We have a great deal to learn about
our utter weakness, and, consequently, about the
need of deliverance. So we are elect unto the
obedience of Christ, and are sprinkled with the blood
of Jesus, which gives us the comfortable assurance
that our sins are clean gone. Hence the difference
is very plain.

Now these " dreamers " referred to, lived in the
imagination of their own hearts, and the New Testament is used to help these men very much indeed.
When the New Testament is taken up by the natural
mind, they proclaim what is called Christian
Socialism, which sets up a standard of the gospel and
dictates to everybody. You have no right to this
large property ! You have no right to these privileges
that you assume ! I am as good as you, and better
too ! This is the style these men take up with regard
to the New Testament, thereby entirely twisting the
word in order to gain advantages to themselves and
to deny all the truth. It is really dreaming about
what ought to be, according to their mind, and to
claim everything that they covet from those that

are in a dignified position in the world—" likewise also these dreamers defile the flesh, despise dominion and speak evil of dignities." They defile the flesh by what they convert scripture to. They consider themselves the equals of all, and not only so, but speak evil of dignities, so that there is evidently no fear of God before their eyes at all. And this shows that there is something very lamentable in the perversion of the gospel, the perversion of the New Testament. It is their own bad and selfish purpose that causes them to do this. The whole principle of the New Testament is this : what those that are of Christ do. Well, they feel according to Christ. What is that ? Why, it is the principle of love that gives, that does not seek its own. Do you think these kind of men have any idea of giving? They only talk about other people giving. So this is all dreaming, as it is called here. Very justly Jude launches out into these strong terms, " Likewise also these dreamers defile the flesh, despise dominion, and speak evil of dignities."

VERSE 9

" But Michael the archangel, when contending with the devil he disputed about the body of Moses, durst not bring against him a railing accusation, but said, The Lord rebuke thee " (ver. 9).

The verse now before us presents one ground of exception taken against the Epistle by men who trust

themselves. This introduction of Michael the
archangel seems to them altogether inexplicable,
as they consider it a mere tradition of the Jews
reproduced by Jude or at any rate by one who
wrote the Epistle bearing his name ; for they really
do not know or care who wrote it. Only nobody
must believe that Jude wrote it ! Such talk consists
simply of the objections of unbelief, which, doubting
all that is inspired of God, sets itself to shake the
confidence of those who do believe.

Although it is a fact presented in no other part of
God's word, what solid reason is there in that to
object ? There is ground for thankfulness that He
makes it known here.

Not a few statements may be traced in scripture,
which have been given but a single mention ; but
they are just as certain as any others which are
repeatedly named. The apostle Paul, in 1 Cor. vi. 3,
declares that the saints shall judge angels. It is not
only that they shall judge the world, which no
doubt is a truth revealed elsewhere ; but it is
there expressly said that they are to judge angels. I
am not aware of any other scripture which intimates
a destiny that most would consider strange if not
incredible. We do find that the world to come is not
to be put under angels ; but that is a different thing.
It does assure us that the habitable earth is to be put
under the Lord Jesus in that day ; and the saints
are to reign with Him. To the risen saints will be
given to share His royal authority ; for that is the

meaning here of " judging." It has nothing at all to
do with Christ's final award of man. It is not a small
mistake to suppose that the saints will exercise the
final judgment over men or angels. All such judgment is exclusively given to the Son of man (John
v. 22, 27 ; Rev. xx.).

When it is said that we shall judge the world,
the meaning is plain whether men believe or not.
Such judging is to exercise the highest power and
authority over the world by the will of God and for
the glory of the Lord Jesus. But there is no warrant
for the notion that saints will take part in the great
white throne judgment. On that throne sits only One,
He that knows every secret, that searches the reins
and hearts ; and He is the sole Judge when it is a
question of judging man in the day when God will
judge the secrets of men by Jesus Christ, according
to Paul's gospel. No man was ever given to fathom
the lives of others ; nor am I aware that we shall
ever be called to share that knowledge so essential
to the Judge of quick and dead.

In fact, the notion that we are to sit in judgment
on people for eternity is a gross and groundless
blunder, for which there is no shadow of proof in
any part of scripture. But we shall judge the world
when the world-kingdom of our Lord and of His
Christ is come. He will reign for ever ; and so shall
we, as His word assures ; but there is a special display of this joint reign, and this is during the thousand years. This, of course, is no question of eternal

judgment, but of the kingdom ; whereas, when the
earth and the heaven flee, and no place is found for
them, eternal judgment follows, and none but the
Lord judges. All judgment is given to Him, when
the works of men, who despised Him throughout the
sad annals of time, come up for His eternal sentence.
No assessors are associated with Him ; He alone
is the Judge.

There remains, however, the plain revelation that
we shall judge angels. If this is confined to that one
scripture, be it so ; one clear word of God is as sure
as a thousand. If we have to do with the witness of
man, the word of a thousand, if they are decent
people, must naturally have a weight beyond one
man's. But here it is no question of men at all.
What we stand upon, and the only thing that gives
us firmness of ground and elevation above all mist,
the only thing that gives us faith, reverence, simplicity, and humility, is God's word. It is indeed a
wonderful mercy, in a world of unbelief, truly to say,
I believe God ; to bow before, and rest in, the testimony of God ; to have perfect confidence in what
God has not only said, but written expressly to arrest,
exercise, and inform our hearts.

Assuredly, if God says a thing once unmistakably,
it is as certain as if it had pleased Him to say it many
times. Indeed, as it appears to me, it will be found
that God hardly ever repeats the same thing. There
is a shade of difference in the different forms that
God takes for communicating truth. Such is one of

its great beauties, though quite lost to unbelievers, because they listen to His words in a vague and uncertain manner. As they never appropriate, so they never hear God in it. They may think of Paul or Peter, John or James, and flatter themselves to be quite as good or perhaps better. What is there in all this but man's exalting himself to his own debasement ? He sinks morally every time he lifts himself up proudly against God and His word.

Here then we have a fact about the unseen world communicated, not in the days of Moses or Joshua, when the burial of Moses is brought before us. Here Jude writes many years after Christ, and first mentions it. Why should this appear strange ? The right moment was come for God's good pleasure to communicate it.

Did not the apostle Paul first give us in his last Epistle the names of the Egyptian magicians who opposed Moses before Pharaoh ? No doubt we were told of such magicians ; but we did not know their names till the Second Epistle to Timothy was written. Scripture can only be resolved into the will of God. It pleases God to exercise His entire sovereignty in this, and He would therein show Paul given to write of a thing reserved for him to bring out alone. So here we have the Holy Ghost proving His power and wisdom in recalling a mysterious fact at the close of Moses' life. Why should men doubt what is so easy for God to make known ?

Is there anything too wonderful for His grace ?

Is not He Who works in revealing, God's eternal
Spirit ?   And why should not He, if He see fit,
reserve the names for that day when Paul wrote ?
The occasion was the growth of deceivers in Christendom—a thing that many seem disposed to entirely
overlook. They yield to the amiable fancy that such
an evil is impossible, especially among the brethren !
But why so ? Surely such impressions are not only
stupid in the highest degree, but unbelieving too.
It ought to be evident that, if anywhere on the face
of the earth Satan would work mischief, it is exactly
among such as stand for God's word and Spirit.
Where superstition is tolerated, and rationalism
reigns, he has already gained ruinous advantage
over the religious and the profane. If any on the
face of the earth at the present time refute both
these hateful yet imposing errors, his spite must be
against them. The reason is plain. We have no
confidence in the flesh, but in the Lord ; and to that
one Name we are gathered for all we boast, leaning
only on His word and the Spirit of God.

Let these then be our Jachin and Boaz, the two
pillars of God's house, even in a day of ruin and
scattering. Let us rejoice to be despised for the
truth's sake. How can we expect to have any other
feelings excited towards us ? Do we not tell everybody that the church is a wreck outwardly ? And
do they not say on the contrary that the church bids
fair for reunion ? that the classes and the masses
are alike won by grand buildings, rites, ceremonies,

music, and the like ? that there is on the one side inflexible antiquity for those who venerate the past, but on the other side the device of development to flatter the hopeful and self-confident ? Then think of the modern influx of gold and silver, of which the apostolic church was so short ! Is it not God now giving it to His church that they may in time buy up the world ! And if any tell them that all such vaunts are only among the proofs of the church's utter ruin, what can they be but hateful and obnoxious in their eyes ? Christ has always a path for the saints, a way of truth, love, and holiness for the darkest day of ruin, as much as for any other. It is for the eye single to Him and the ear that heeds His word to find the path, narrow as it is, but its lines fallen in pleasant places and a goodly heritage. But if we, hankering after earthly things, entangle ourselves with man's thoughts or the world's ways in religion, what can this issue be but that we help on the ruin ? Disturbed, uneasy and unhappy we become, like Samson with his hair cut, weak as water, and blind to boot.

Nor is it at all unaccountable that men are busy against an Epistle which is one of the loudest and clearest in the trumpet blast that is blown against Christendom. For it expressly lays down that departure from the truth, and the turning God's grace to licentiousness, are to go on till judgment thereon— not that there may not be such as are faithful and true, keeping themselves in the love of God, and

building themselves up on that most holy faith that
was once for all delivered to the saints. What can
be conceived more remote from men's new inventions ? from the vain restlessness which is ever in
quest of some fresh effort ? From everything of the
sort we are bound to keep clear, as being deadly. It
is not only from all tampering with bad ways, or
false doctrine, but from humanising on what is
divine. To this we are bound by the very nature of
Christianity, which calls us to entire dependence
upon the word and Spirit of God. It is not for us
then, to be asking what is the wrong of this ? or
what harm is there in that ? For the believer the
true question is, What saith the scripture ? How
is it written ?

It is written here : " But Michael the archangel,
when, contending with the devil, he disputed about
the body of Moses, durst not bring against him a
railing accusation, but said, The Lord rebuke thee "
(ver. 9). Here, then, is a grand truth, taught in a
striking and powerful manner. The apostle Peter,
in the 2nd chapter of his Second Epistle, is said to
give exactly the same thing as Jude, but he says
not one word about it. He makes no allusion to
Michael the archangel. He speaks in verse 4 of angels
that sinned, whom God did not spare. But Jude
presents it as the angels that kept not their first
estate. This clearly has nothing to do with Michael.
The reference to the archangel is entirely peculiar to
Jude ; and the object is to exhibit the spirit that

becomes one who acts for God, even in dealing with His worst enemy, that there be no meeting evil with evil, nor reviling with reviling, but on the contrary immediate and confessed reference to God.

What makes it all the more surprising is the power vouchsafed to Michael. He is the angel whom God will employ to overthrow the devil from his evil eminence by-and-by (Rev. xii.). But here the historical intimation given is entirely in character with the future. You may tell me that Rev. xii. was not revealed to Jude, who wrote this. Be it so, yet the same God that wrought by Jude wrought also by John. It is evident from the two scriptures that the antagonism between Michael and the devil is not a truth foreign to God's word. There we have it in the written word. It is the truth of God. Jude was given to tell us what God moved Jude to write, which has not only great moral value for any time, but gives us the fact, full of interest, that the antagonism between Michael the archangel and the devil is not merely of the future. Here the proof lies before us that it wrought also in the past. Thus we can look back fifteen hundred years, and there behold the evidence of this contention between the devil and the archangel. Do you say that it was about the body of Moses, and what is that to anyone ? Can we not readily enter into the importance of that dispute ? Can we not understand the bearing of that question, when we hold in mind all the history

of Israel in the wilderness, as given in Exodus and
Numbers ?

There is nothing more common among the prophets than this, that while during their lifetime
they were hated, after they were dead and gone
they became objects of the highest honour ; and,
what is so remarkable, the highest honour to the
same class of people that hated them. They became
not objects of honour so much to other people, but
were honoured by the same unbelieving class that
could not endure the prophets' words when they
were alive. They are ready to kill the prophetic
messenger when living, and all but worship him
when he is dead. Well, it is the same unbelief that
acts in both ways ; which, when he was alive,
scouted the word of God come through him, and
condemned and hated him, but when he was dead,
and no longer, therefore, a living character to
puncture their conscience, the very people who had
war with the prophet would build a fine monument
to his memory ; and so, getting the character of
being men who had a great regard for the prophet,
men, therefore, that were doing their best for
religion, they gave their money to have erected a
fine monument, or to have a fine statue made, or as
grand a picture as they could pay for ! So true it is,
the flesh is quite remarkable for being ready to
honour a man when he is dead and gone, whom it
could not endure when alive. Our Lord drew attention to this very characteristic. It is not an idea of

mine at all, it is the truth of God. Our Lord lays
this down most strongly against the Jewish people ;
and it is not at all confined to Jewish people. If you
go now to the town of Bedford—to take an instance
from our own country—there you will find a fine
monument to John Bunyan, who, when alive, was
scouted, imprisoned, and regarded as a presump-
tuous, bad man. The very same class of people now
buy his book, and at any rate are not sorry that
the children should read it along with the *Arabian
Nights' Entertainments* in the nursery. So there
they have the *Pilgrim's Progress* and the *Arabian
Nights'* tales, and they are all considered equally
entertaining for the children. They thereby show
that they think the imprisoned tinker was a genius—
for that is their way of looking at it ; and therefore
they gain for themselves credit in all sorts of ways,
both as being men of taste, and also as men not at all
averse to religion when it does not touch their conscience. The thing, therefore, that I am speaking of
is always true and always will be true till the Lord
come, and then there will be no such thing as " the
vile person called liberal, nor the churl said to be
bountiful," nor, on the other hand, the unjust
treated as righteous. Then there will be righteousness reigning, and everything and everyone will find
their level according to God.

Now we all know from the account given of
Moses, both in Exodus and Numbers, how constantly
the children of Israel were contending with him,

murmuring against him, speaking evil of him—
hating Moses, really, and Aaron too. And it was
only the power of God interfering every now and
then that alarmed them, and cut them down, and
compelled them at any rate to pay outward respect.
But directly he was dead, the same devil that stirred
them up against Moses when he was alive—oh, what
would he not have given for that dead body ! The
dead body would have been made a relic. You know
very well that this is a favourite idea of men—the
dead body would have been an object of worship.
The devil would, therefore, have gained doubly.
First, by setting them at war with him while alive,
and still more when he was dead by making them
idolaters of Moses. So that we can easily understand
why it was that the Lord buried the body Himself.
But it appears that before he was buried, there was
this contention between Michael the archangel and
the devil about Moses' dead body ; so perfectly in
keeping with the mysterious manner in which
Jehovah buried him where none should know, and
where even if Satan was allowed to know, God inter-
fered that Michael should guard that grave, that
Michael should hinder all the efforts of the devil to
get hold of that dead body. So we have the two facts :
what is here told us by Jude, and the fact of the
xxxivth of Deuteronomy, where we have the account
of the Lord's burying Moses—which He never did
for any other man. Show me only a single case of the
Lord's burying any one. I do not remember one but

that of Moses, and there were special reasons why
Jehovah should secretly bury that dead body rather
than any other.

There never was a man that exercised so remarkable a position towards a whole people as Moses did
to the children of Israel, and now that he was gone,
a reaction would take place under the devil, not in
the least a reaction of faith, but of unbelief, to idolise
that very body, the same man whom they continually plagued while living.

So that the fact, here brought before us, goes
along with another fact to which I have just now
referred in the Old Testament (the two perfectly
tally), *viz.*—that there were special reasons in the
case of Moses' dead body why the Lord should interfere. Now we learn from this passage in Jude a
further very interesting fact, not about the Lord,
but about the enemy and the one whom Jehovah
thought proper to use. Now, there are others of great
weight in heaven besides Michael. Gabriel stands in
the presence of God, and, as we know, he was employed for a very important mission by God. It
was not Michael, but Gabriel very particularly,
who was used in announcing the birth of our Lord
Jesus, and we can perfectly understand why Gabriel
should be then employed rather than Michael.
Michael is the prince that stands up for the Jewish
people. Yes, but the Gospel of Luke shows the Lord
Jesus born of woman, not merely for the Jewish
people, but for man—" God's good pleasure in

men," not merely in Jews : and therefore it is not
that particular angel, Michael ; he was not employed
on that occasion. So that it appears to me that there
was divine wisdom in Gabriel being employed on that
mission rather than Michael ; and that this is true
will surely be very evident to anyone who reads
the xth and xiith chapters of the book of Daniel.
I just refer to it now because of its importance in
showing the harmony of scripture, and that even in
a most extraordinary event that is only once
recorded. It shows principles of divine truth that
support, and fall in, and harmonise, with what
was only revealed once. This is what I wish to
show now.

Well, in the latter part of the xth chapter of
Daniel (indeed as well the xith chapter), ver. 20, we
read, " Then said he " (this is the angel that had to
do with Daniel), " Knowest thou wherefore I come
unto thee ? and now will I return to fight with the
prince of Persia." There you see that it is not quite
an unusual thing for angels to contend. Here we
have it in still stronger language : " To fight
with the prince of Persia : and when I am gone
forth, lo, the prince of Grecia shall come."

Now, we shall find a little intimation who and
what these princes were in the next verse : " But
I will show thee that which is noted in the scripture
of truth : and there is none that holdeth with me in
these things, but Michael your prince."

We learn here that Michael was pre-eminently the

prince of Israel. In what sense? Not as reigning
visibly, but as invisibly espousing the cause of the
Jewish people. Now see how this falls in with
Michael's guarding the dead body of Moses, with his
being employed by God to contend with the great
enemy, so that there should be no misuse made of
that dead body. Who had so pre-eminently this
duty as the prince of Israel? And as to the angel
that was speaking with Daniel, of whom we read a
good deal in the previous part of the chapter in so
highly interesting a manner and in the most glowing
colours—he says, " there is none that holdeth with
me in these things "—that is, in opposing the
princes of Grecia and Persia. Why? It appears that
the princes of Grecia and Persia were not favourable
to the Jewish people. In the same way, they had
interests connected with Greece and Persia that were
opposed to the Jewish people ; and in the providence
of God the angels are referred to here—angels are
the great instruments of providence, the unseen
working of God being carried out instrumentally by
angels.

This is true now. We are all very much cared for
by the angels, more than we are apt to think. We
read of them in Hebrews (chap. i. 14) : " Are they
not all ministering spirits, sent forth to minister
for them who shall be heirs of salvation ? " So we
are indebted to angels now. I do not say it is Michael
or Gabriel, but I do say that the angels are acting
a special part at this present time in Christianity for

all the heirs of salvation. You see that at this time, in Daniel, it was not so much a question about the heirs of salvation ; it was a question of the Jewish people. They were the great object of God's care in their fallen estate. They had been most guilty, but they were beloved. They were carried into captivity by the Babylonian power. And they were going to be the slaves of other powers on the earth ; but for all that Michael stood up for them and this other angel who speaks to the prophet Daniel. There were also other angels that were opposed, whom they had to fight.

Well, people may say that it is all very mysterious. Indeed it is, dear brethren. It is not, therefore, incredible, but of very great moment, that we should have our hearts and minds open to believe what we do not see. There is nothing that adds more to the simplicity of a believer than his having his faith exercised upon the things that are unseen as well as those that are eternal, and we ought to feel our indebtedness to God for these things.

Now, if you want a proof even in detail as to this, take the viiith chapter of the Acts of the Apostles. There you find that the angel tells Philip to go in a certain direction, and he does so ; and then we find the Spirit speaks. Not the angel, but the Spirit. I had better refer to it, because there is nothing like the scripture for its precision. Now, in Acts viii. 26 we read : " And the angel of the Lord spake unto Philip, saying, Arise and go toward the south

unto the way that goeth down from Jerusalem
unto Gaza, which is desert." There were two roads,
it appears. One was through a populous part of the
land, and the other was desert. Well, a desert is not
the place an evangelist would choose. The angel,
therefore, acting in the providence of God, says to
Philip : " You go that desert road." And it is one
of the beautiful features of Philip that he was not a
reasoner. Reason is an excellent thing for men who
have not got the word of God, and I do not say that
there may not be useful reasoning outside divine
things, what you may call common sense. But I do
say this, that the more the believer can act on divine
principles at all times, the better for his soul, and the
more to the praise of the Lord. If he is sometimes
acting, like a man of the world, on his common
sense, and at another time acting on the word of
God as a believer, he is in danger of being practically
two different persons. And when a man plays the
game of two personalities he is very apt to become a
hypocrite ; there will be a want of reality about the
man. We ought only to have one personality. We
are bought with a price, not merely for our religious
matters, but for everything. We do not belong to
ourselves, we are the Lord's ; and, therefore, the
more a believer can rise above merely what he will
do as a man to that which he loves to do as a saint—
the more entirely he keeps to this only, so much
the more consistent is he with his profession as a
child of God. For why should it not be so ? What is

to hinder his being a saint in anything at all?
Cannot he be a saint when serving in his shop?
Cannot he be a saint when in his office? Surely
he might, and ought to be. There is nothing to
hinder, if he were lively in faith and has the Lord
before him. But if, on the contrary, he only looks
at the shop or the office—" Well, now," he says,
" it is not Sunday, nor is it the meeting now; I
go there as a man." So there it is. How can he
expect anything like faith, or grace, care for Christ
and His glory, if that is the case? I deny entirely
that we may not be servants of Christ in the com-
monest things of this life; and this is what, I think,
we have all especially to pray for. Of course, we
need to pray that we may behave as saints when we
come into the assembly, and when we find ourselves
at a meeting of any kind; but why we should be off
our saintship when we go into business or anything
else is another matter, and a very dangerous line to
pursue.

Now then, here you see that we have the angel of
the Lord providentially dealing with Philip, and
Philip acts upon it at once. He does not say, " Ah,
I shall not be able to get a congregation, and at any
rate I don't like a little one; I want to have a big
one." He has not a word about little or big; in
fact, he was not going to have a congregation. He
must be content with one single soul. That soul is
precious beyond all calculation to God, if not even
to himself. What would all the world be to one if the

soul were lost, as the Lord Himself told men, and
which they still refuse to believe ?

Well then, the angel gives Philip this word, and
he hears, and goes without a question. But when he
was there—in this road, " this way that goeth down
from Jerusalem "—here this Ethiopian stranger in
his chariot was met, returning from Jerusalem, and
reading the prophet Isaiah. He was not now going
up to Jerusalem to get a blessing there. He may
have looked for and prayed for that, but he did not
get it there.   He was returning from Jerusalem
unblest, going away from that city, and this was
just what the gospel was doing. It was leaving
Jerusalem, driven out by unbelief, and this poor
Jewish proselyte was going away unblest by the
gospel in that city, for he had not found a blessing
there. There was a persecution going on there against
it.   And now, returning, he was reading in his
chariot. " Then the Spirit said unto Philip, Go near
and join thyself to this chariot." Now, why is it the
Spirit here ?   Because it was what concerned the
word of God and the soul. The angel said not a word
about the soul of the Ethiopian. I do not know that
the angel knew anything about it. The angel had to
do the bidding of God, " Tell that man to go by the
road that is a desert." He acted on it ; the angel
was right, and Philip was right, but it was entirely
providential.   And then comes the spiritual part,
and here the Holy Ghost interposes.

Well, we have not now the angel speaking and the

Holy Ghost speaking, but we have the angels acting.
We may not perhaps know how it is, but an angel
interposes many a time to prevent us going in a
certain way, when, if there had not been that inter-
position, we should have been killed. We often go
where we had no intention of going, or do not go
where we meant to go. When I say " often," I
mean sometimes ; throughout our whole lives it
would really bear the word " often." But there is
no man but what does from time to time what he
never intended to do, perhaps through an impulse
given him—he cannot tell how or why—and he goes
this way, when he meant to have gone that way.

   Here, however, we find that there is another kind
of guidance of a more spiritual nature for the soul,
prompting (so to speak) the soul to give a word for
the Lord. Do you suppose there is no such thing
now ? Such an idea may be for people who do not
believe that the Holy Ghost is come, and that to
abide ; but He is still here. It is put in Acts viii.
in an open objective form, but it is meant to teach
us that the same thing is true now, although it does
not come out openly in the same manner. It is
quite true, and this is not the only case. If you
compare the xiith chapter of the Acts with the
xiiith, you will see an angel acting in the one chapter
and the Spirit acting in the next. I only mention
it because the Acts of the Apostles is surely a
history of Christianity, a history of Christians, of
what Christians have been used for, and what they

are meant to live in. Well, then, here, when it was
not a question of Christians or the gospel, but of
nations and people, we find the part that the angels
play—not merely the holy ones, but the unholy
ones. This is the very thing that we find at the
grave of Moses, and about that same people, Israel.
Michael is the prince who stands up for them
opposing the efforts of the enemy against them ;
and this entirely confirms the principles of God's
word. They are entirely in favour of this extraordinary revelation made in the 9th verse of Jude,
and they are found to support and confirm it in the
highest degree.

Now, before we go further, I refer to another
scripture in Zechariah iii. There we have a very
interesting removal of the veil that we may see the
unseen. We read these words : " And he showed
me " (that is, the angel showed Zechariah) " Joshua
the high priest standing before the angel of Jehovah,
and Satan standing at his right hand to resist him "
(ver. 1). There you have the same opposition again.
In this case, however, it is the " angel of Jehovah."
I should be disposed to distinguish him from Michael.
The " angel of Jehovah " is an altogether peculiar
term. The angel of Jehovah is rather the way in
which the Lord Jesus is referred to in the Old
Testament—not the only way, but a very usual way.
The angel of Jehovah every now and then is shown
to be Jehovah Himself. I do not mean that He is
the only person that is Jehovah. As we read in

Deut. vi. 4, " Jehovah our God is one Jehovah,"
that is, it is Father, Son and Holy Spirit, Who are
the one God that we acknowledge as Christians.
They are all three Jehovah, they are all equally
Jehovah, and it therefore helps us to understand why
He is viewed as " the Angel of Jehovah." He is
Jehovah too, though not the only One that is called
Jehovah. This explains what we have here : " He
showed me Joshua the high priest standing before
the angel of Jehovah, and Satan standing at his
right hand to resist him. And Jehovah " (notice
that after speaking of " the angel of Jehovah " it is
now " Jehovah ")—" And Jehovah said unto Satan,
Jehovah rebuke thee, O Satan "—the very words
that Michael uses to Satan as reported by Jude !

Well, is not this a very strong confirmation, not
only of this remarkable opposition between the holy
angels and the unholy ones, but also of Satan's
opposition ? We find this antagonism in both
scriptures, precisely alike. Even Jehovah Himself,
instead of merely taunting Satan, says " Jehovah
rebuke thee." The time was not yet for the most
terrible rebuke to come, as it will unmistakably
when he shall be trodden under foot. He has to be
bound for a thousand years in the abyss ; he has to
be cast into the lake of fire. All these will be
part of the ways in which Jehovah will rebuke him,
but till that time arrives we see how God meanwhile
guards His own purpose ; He does not allow Satan
to interfere with His design. He allows man to

show out his insensibility and his sin, and He chastises him. He does not yet put forth His power to deal with Satan as He will do ; but there is that word, " Jehovah rebuke thee," as He surely will. It is a continual warning from Jehovah, which will be accomplished in its own day, and in various places and various stages. But you can easily see that it would be unseemly to have a mere dispute going on between Jehovah and Satan ; and all, therefore, that He puts forth is this solemn warning of what is coming.

Well, the angel repeats that warning to Satan in a very early day, and here, a thousand years after, you have the same truth, the same antagonism even, if not the same persons exactly ; but the same spirit all through.

Scripture is perfectly consistent, perfectly reliable. And although Jude was the first one that brought out this fact, it falls in with the other facts of scripture : both in the early days of Moses, in the later of Zechariah, and now in the days of the gospel, in the days of Christianity.

So that nothing can be more complete than the proof that these learned critics are totally ignorant of God, totally ignorant of the Bible, except of the mere surface, the mere letter that kills, and know not the spirit that quickens.

Well, here then you see how beautiful it is that instead of bringing a railing accusation, Michael simply warned Satan with the solemn words :

" Jehovah rebuke thee "—" The Lord rebuke thee."
What would railing do ? If there are two people
railing, a good and a bad man, and the bad man's
railing provokes the good man to rail, the good
man goes down to the level of the bad. It does not
at all diminish the railing of the other. I should
think at any time that a bad man could gain a good
degree over the good man in the way of railing.
Surely he is much more practised, and very likely
more unscrupulous and more malicious, and therefore
it sounds stronger to the ear of man. But, you see,
that would be a total lowering of even an angel,
and how much more of a saint, I might say. Here
we have the beautiful conduct of the angel as a
pattern to the saint, that we be not provoked, nor,
when we are reviled, revile again, but act as the
Lord Himself acted. He committed Himself to
Him that judgeth righteously. Well, that is what
Jehovah will do ; He will judge righteously, but
the time is not yet come for its manifestation.

VERSES 10-13

" BUT these rail at whatever things they know
not ; but whatever they understand naturally, as
the irrational animals, in these things they corrupt
themselves (or, perish). Woe unto them ! because
they went in the way of Cain, and rushed greedily
into the error of Balaam's hire, and perished in
the gainsaying of Korah " (vers. 10, 11).

" But these speak evil "—referring now to the persons who, notwithstanding that they had been baptised and had taken their place in the church, were now yielding to every form of corruption, were abandoning the very things that they professed. I do not say that they were outside. This is the difference between Jude and John. When we come down to John's Epistle they went out ; but the corrupting thing in Jude is that there they are poisoning others.

Now it is remarkable that in the Second Epistle of Peter we have only Balaam, and Michael we have not at all ; so that nothing can be more superficial than the idea that the one writer has copied the other. It is true that there is much that is common to both Epistles, but the *differences* between Jude and Peter are the striking thing ; the points of resemblance are easily accounted for. In the position in which Jude and Peter were, there must have been the closest friendship, and a very near companionship ; and there must have been strong links of love between these two elder servants of the Lord. Would they not communicate their thoughts and judgments to each other, even if they are looked at as servants of God ? This is nothing, therefore, at all surprising. Nothing more likely than that Peter should communicate a good deal to Jude, and, on the other hand, that Jude should communicate a good deal to Peter ; and, besides, the Spirit of God giving them to look at the same, or kindred evil, would give them similar judgments and thoughts. You find that in people who have never met or spoken to one another, if they have to do with the same evil, they often say things very much alike ; substantially alike they are sure to be, if guided by the Spirit of God, but there are often surprising verbal resemblances. But this is not where the beauty and the striking nature of the two Epistles of Jude and of Second Peter show themselves. It is in the differences between them.

Now Peter is particularly occupied with wicked teachers—men that privily brought in, what he calls, " heresies," or sects. The word " heresy " in scripture means " a sect." It never means hetero-doxy, as we use the word in its modern sense. That is not the scriptural sense at all. No doubt in the sect there might be heterodoxy, and there might be a sect without heterodoxies, or there might be one with a great deal of heterodoxy. So that " sect " admits of all kinds, or shades, of evil and error ; but Peter is looking particularly at false teachers, and these false teachers covetous men ; greed of gain is one marked feature which he specifies. Well now, where could you get an Old Testament example of greed so marked as Balaam ? Consequently, we find Balaam in Peter, just where it should be. It falls in entirely with his purport, and with that Second Epistle and second chapter.

But here, Jude, in this very much shorter Epistle— and far more compact, far more compressed, and

far more vehement—writes as in a tempest of hatred
of all these bad men.   Indeed, I do not know stronger
language.   Some do not like strong language.   But
that should entirely depend upon how it is used.
Strong language against what is good is infamous,
but against what is bad is thoroughly right ; and I
do not know stronger language anywhere than in
this very Epistle of Jude in which he speaks out
against railing.   But strong language and railing
are not the same thing.   Railing is abuse of what is
good ; but here we have the pithiest, the most
vehement, and most cutting exposure of what is
evil ; and instead of this being a thing to regret, it is
a thing that we ought to feel and go along with
heartily.   But I know it does not suit the present
age.   The present age is an age for trying to think
that there is nothing so good but what there is
bad in it, and nothing so bad but what there is
good in it.   The consequence is that all moral
power is at a deadlock, and people have no real,
burning love for what is good—only a calm, quiet,
lukewarm state.   They are neither strong for good
nor strong against evil ; and that is a state which, I
believe, the Lord hates—at any rate, it does not
agree with either Peter or Jude.

"Woe unto them ! because they went in the
way of Cain, and rushed greedily into the error of
Balaam's hire, and perished in the gainsaying of
Korah."   In the Epistle of Peter there is not a word
about Cain, not a word about Korah.   But here

you see that Jude, having a different object,
compresses in this most wonderful verse—for it is a
most wonderful verse—an amount of moral truth,
spiritual truth, divine truth, that was here entirely
departed from, grace being altogether hated and
abused. All this is found in this short verse. He
goes up to Cain.

" These are spots (or, hidden rocks) in your
love-feasts, feasting together, fearlessly pasturing
themselves ; clouds without water, carried along
by winds ; autumnal trees without fruit, twice dead,
rooted up ; raging sea-waves, foaming out their own
shames ; wandering stars for whom hath been
reserved the gloom of darkness for ever " (vers.
12, 13).

I cannot conceive any but an inspired man
venturing to use such decided and solemn language
about those that were within the church. That is a
marked point of the Epistle. Peter looks at the
unrighteousness of man generally, even since
Christianity is come, because he is occupied simply
with iniquity. This of course is common to both
writers ; but Jude looks specially at those who took
the place of salvation, those that were gathered
to the name of the Lord. In this latter case, therefore, the matter had yet more seriousness for the
spiritual mind. There is nothing more dangerous
than a departure from the faith, the Christian faith.
It is not only what man is and has done, but also
what grace has made known, for which we are

responsible, most of all if we turn from it in unbelief. What is so evil as apostasy ?

There are many things that cause truth to lose its power with men. Nothing hastens it more than moral disorder in ourselves, which results from forgetting or abusing grace. We turn our backs on God's authority, as well as our relation to our Lord Jesus ; this is followed by our taking up objects that are loved so as to become practically our idols. It is clear that these things have been substantially so from the beginning, as it is also clear from this Epistle that things will go on worse and worse, until the Lord comes in judgment. As to this point we shall have to weigh what is yet stronger than what we have already considered, when it will be ours to seek a divine impression of the words already read. Manifestly they are of the darkest character and full of energy.

Observe here the word, " Woe." I do not know it anywhere in the New Testament except in the very different application which the apostle makes to himself, if he did not make the glad tidings known (1 Cor. ix. 16).   Here it is, " Woe unto them." I am not of course speaking of the Gospels, but of the Epistles; where the Spirit of God is testifying of the Saviour and His work to man, or dealing with those who bear the Lord's name. In the Gospels, even our Lord could not but say, " Woe " ; but then He was warning those that represented a favoured nation, which was then through unbelief passing under divine judgment. The same One Who began His ministry with Blessed, blessed, blessed, ended it with Woe, woe, woe ! Nothing was further from His heart than to pronounce that sentence, but as He said, so was He to execute it in due time. He pronounced it as a Prophet when on the earth, if peradventure they might take it to heart, and He will pronounce it as a Judge on the great white throne when heaven and earth pass away.

What, then, is the explanation of this utterance of Paul, " Woe unto me if I preach not the gospel " ? Paul, who had been a poor deluded soul, by the grace of God had a fearful warning to do His will in preaching, but he does not say " Woe " to them, like Jude. He might have had his great fears for some when he let the Corinthians know how possible it was for a man who preached the gospel nevertheless to become a reprobate (1 Cor. ix. 27). I think there is no doubt that that word " reprobate " means one lost ; because salvation does not go with preaching, it goes with believing ; and it is quite possible for those who preach to destroy the faith which once they preached. We have known that ourselves from time to time, and it has always been so. But the apostle had such a solemn sense of his responsibility to proclaim the gospel to perishing souls everywhere, that " Woe unto me if I preach not the gospel." Yet he preached it in the spirit of grace beyond any man that ever lived.

Here, however, in Jude it is a very different case. " Woe unto them," he says, " for they have gone in the way of Cain, and run greedily after the error of Balaam for reward, and perished in the gainsaying of Korah."

It is a most remarkable picture of the history of Christendom on its blackest side. There cannot be anything more graphic. It is not the mere order of history. If it were the order of history then the error of Balaam would be put last. It is a moral order, the order of men's souls. It is what presented itself to the apostle in the Holy Ghost. Jude begins with the first root of what is wrong, and I think he is referring to a man (Cain) that ought to be a brother in affection, and who ought to have been a holy brother, because he took the place of being a worshipper. Cain brought his offering to Jehovah, and it was that very bringing of his offering to Jehovah that brought out his wickedness. How little people know what may be the turning-point of ruin for their souls ! Cain no doubt went forward with confidence and with a step of assurance in his offering of fine fruit and other productions of the earth that he had cultivated, no doubt, with care. We may be sure he had chosen the very best because *man* would not fail in that. A man of the world is often very careful indeed as to outward appearances. Cain sees nothing defective in the offering itself—in the materials that composed the offering ; but there was this vital defect which completely ruined him,

that there was no faith. There is no mention of
either God on the one hand, which must be, nor,
on the other hand, was there any judgment of his
own sinfulness. He failed therefore completely as
to the inner man, for God never calls upon men
who put on any *appearance* before Him. This is
what was done here ; perhaps no great depth of it,
but still Cain took the place of a worshipper and he
brought his offering to Jehovah, with no conscious-
ness of his own ruin by sin, nor of God's grace, or of
the need of it. But that was not all.

On the same occasion, Abel brought his offering,
which was acceptable ; his offering was of the
first-born of the flock. Not only was it blood that
he offered, the acknowledgment of the necessity of
death, and of the Saviour to meet his sins, but there
was also the sense of the excellency of the Saviour
before God—he brought " of the fat thereof."
Consequently there was a most decided effect in
the case of Abel when he brought his offering before
God. His very name shows what was very true of
his character, no confidence in himself, for the
word " Abel " refers to that which passes away like
smoke, whereas " Cain " has the signification of
" acquisition," very much like the word " gain " in
our language. Abel was a man entirely dependent
upon grace, upon the Seed of the woman of whom he
had no doubt heard over and over again from both
father and mother, with other truths which he had
never forgotten. God took care that these truths

should be most prominent from the very earliest day, but it made no impression on Cain, and the reason was because he had never judged himself before God, and had no sense of his real need whatever. The opposite of all this was true of Abel, and his offering Jehovah accepted. This at once drew out the character of Cain ; plain enough before to God, but it now came out openly in his hatred of his brother. What had his brother done to arouse that wickedness ? You may be sure that the general character produced by faith in Abel had shown itself in every way of tender affection to his elder brother ; but Cain could not brook that God should accept Abel and his offering, and not look at Cain's. Nevertheless God deigned to expostulate with him and his lack of faith, in order to save him, if it could be, from what his wicked heart was rushing into. But no ; Cain failed both before God and man, and what is more, before his brother. Now this is the first great beginning of the ruin of Christendom, and this showed itself in early days. We find such a thing quite common in our own days. We cannot doubt but that there was a powerful impression made on the world by the new life and ways of real Christians ; yet there always were persons who have not only no sympathy with God's love, but who even despise it, and who are irritated by it, more especially if they are dealt with faithfully by those that know it. This is another reason why our minds are blinded towards our brothers. There

comes a still worse feeling towards God, but this
order was reversed in Cain's case. In the root of
the matter, I suppose that all evil feeling towards
one another springs from a previous feeling towards
God. Our feeling in the presence of God breaks
out in the presence of one another. Certainly this
was the case with Cain.

Here we find the first woe. " Woe unto them !
for they have gone in the way of Cain." It is a
departure from faith, it is a departure from love,
it is a departure from righteousness. It was the
spirit of a worldly man, and therefore he was the
first man who began open worldliness. Before that
time there was great simplicity. It would be very
untrue to say that there was the least of what was
savage in Adam and Eve. There was everything
that was sweet and beautiful in what God gave them ;
but still there were not the delights of civilisation,
there was none of those things that people seem
particularly to enjoy in modern times. It cannot be
wise to disguise from our eyes that the progress of
worldliness is enormous. I do not doubt that all
the recent discoveries of gold and silver have
greatly added both to the covetousness of men,
and the desire for " display " one before another
according to their means ; whereas Christianity has
nothing at all to do with " means " ; it has everything to do with faith. If we care to do so there is
always a use for what God gives, that is, to use it to
His glory ; but to turn it all to a selfish account, or

to a display before others, is a mere vulgar kind of selfishness. This is the kind of thing that we find in Cain. There were, of course, the pleasures of stringed and wind instruments from the very beginning of civic life, and there was also then the beauty of poetry, which began, no doubt, rather poorly. It was all man, and man's reasoning. This is all man's enjoyment, and it is practically very much what we have at the present day. No doubt many things have been invented since the early times. There is always development in human things, and there is our development in divine things, but there is no obedience in development. There is nothing divine in development, but there *is* obedience in doing what the Lord sets before us in His word ; yet the moment you add to that word in any way, or take away from it, it is the reverse of God's teaching. It is setting up to be wiser than God, and this we can do without His power. All this idea that we can do something that will do His work better is the work of unbelief, and is an idea destructive of a Christian's peace, and destructive of the simple principle of obedience contained in the word of God. Oh, what a privilege it is to own and teach this principle ! to hear and do His will ! We are always learners, and should we not always be coming to a better knowledge of the word by faith ? Where there is not faith we do not come to this knowledge.

However, we see in the case of Cain a very fit

and proper beginning of the woe that is coming on
and the terrible sin that calls for the woe. Now the
solemn thing is that it also refers to the present
time. Evil never dies out, but gets darker and more
opposed to God—becomes more hardened against
God, without the least compunction of conscience.

Taking events out of mere historical order so as
to make them exactly suit the truth, we have, as
the next thing, the case of Balaam. The incident
which brought out the nature of Balaam and the
fact of his being a typical enemy of God is a further
sample of what was to be in Christendom. This
was when he uttered the most glorious truths ; and
I suppose, they were the only truths which he had
ever uttered in his life. Well, Balaam was drawn to
curse Israel, and he was induced to do so by the
offers of gold and silver and honour of every kind.
And I will even say that he tried to make out that
he did not care for money ; he said he was entirely
above such a paltry consideration. The sin of
Balaam is a very solemn thing. He went out to
sin, he went out to meet (as our translators have
put it) Jehovah—to " meet the Lord," but there
was nothing of " the Lord " in it, the words being
merely added (Num. xxiii. 15). The fact is, he went
to meet the devil, whom he had been accustomed to
meet. He went out to seek enchantment—that is
the devil, of course. Our translators have put in
" the Lord " (Jehovah), but the fact is it was the
enemy of the Lord, the source of all Balaam's

wickedness and wicked power. Balaam knew that
it was a divine power that compelled him to speak
about what he had no thought of speaking about ;
but when he did so, his vast capacity for eloquence
went along with his speaking.

God did not refuse to allow this man's mind to be
displayed. This is the way in which God sometimes
works by all the writers He employs. The man
must be uncommonly dull not to see a difference of
style in comparing the different books of the Bible.
If it were merely the Spirit of God it would be the
same style in all, but it is the Spirit of God causing
a man to bring out the truth of God and to give it
out with that style and feeling which should justly
accompany it. So in the case of Balaam : although
he was much moved by the thought of dying the
death of the righteous, yet there was not one single
working of his soul in communion with God. He
was the enemy of God, and the one who came to
curse the Israel of God, but he was compelled to
give utterance to most glorious predictions. The
wonderful effusions of this wicked prophet glorified
the coming of the Lord Jesus. There is something
of that kind now in Christendom. Sometimes the
most wicked of men can preach eloquently, and
what is extraordinary too, God has often used the
words of unconverted men for the conversion of
others. I have no doubt that this is the case at the
present time, and it has always been so. Of course,
it is altogether one of the side features of ruin.

The normal manner is for those that are saved to be the messengers of salvation to others.

The error of Balaam was that he was the willing instrument of the devil to destroy Israel, and as he could not curse them he did not give it up, yet it was a vain attempt to do so. Jehovah turned it into a blessing. Balaam thought to employ the women of Moab to draw the Israelites after idolatry. He could not turn Jehovah away from Israel, so he tried to turn Israel away from Jehovah. I have no doubt a great many souls throughout Christendom have been converted by these utterances of Balaam. Balaam's eyes were fixed upon Israel—he wanted to damage them ; they were the people he hated, they were the persons he wished to bring down, they were the persons he maligned and misrepresented with all his might, but he did not know that they were the people of Jehovah. But God knew.

Then with regard to Moses and Aaron : Moses represented God, and Aaron represented the intercession of the grace of God ; but Korah would not submit to such a thing for a moment (Num. xvi.). In the case of Korah, what makes it the more atrocious is that he had a very honourable place ; he belonged to the highest rank of the Levites, to that honoured section of the Levites to which Moses had belonged. Moses had first the call of God, Who lifted him up, beyond all question ; but Korah belonged to the most honoured of the three families

of the Levites who were servants or ministers of
the sanctuary, and, as I have said, Korah belonged
to the highest of the Levites ; but nothing satisfied
him. Why ? Because he hated that Moses should
have a place that belonged to him beyond any other.
Satan blinded his eyes, which he always does so
that people may feel like this. Korah's object was
to achieve what pertained only to Moses and Aaron.
There are always many good reasons for bad things,
and the reasons sound well, but they are words
that strike at God and at Christ. There was a
punishment not only of Korah but also of his
family, other Levites, and all their families. And
the earth opened her mouth and swallowed them up
in a way that had never happened on any other
occasion since the world began. There may have
been something resembling it, as in the case of
Sodom and Gomorrha, where it rained fire and
brimstone and consumed the wicked, but the
converse was the case here. The earth opened and
swallowed them up. We find further a remarkable
thing : the children of Korah were not consumed.
He was the leader of the rebellion against Jehovah,
but God in the midst of His judgment showed
mercy to the sons. They did not perish through the
plague that afterwards set in amongst the congregation. These sons of Korah are referred to in the
Psalms, for there is the fact recorded that there are
" the sons of Korah," and the right persons to sing
such psalms. Well, all these things perish that do

not depend upon the grace of God—things like the error of Korah, things that war against God, that cause all those uprisings of falsehood. I think all such things such as the Oxford movement, are wrong. I do not mean the Ritualistic one only, which is extremely vulgar. But what is the error of the Oxford movement? It is very nearly the same error as Korah's. Korah wanted to be priest as well as minister. That kind of thing is what men are doing now who maintain that they are sacrificing priests. It is true that the sacrifice is a perfect absurdity : the sacrifice is the bread and the wine. How could this be a sacrifice? If they called it an offering it would be a better term ; but they not only call it a sacrifice, but they fully believe that Christ personally enters the bread and the wine. Therefore they are bound to worship the " elements," as they call it. Such an idea is lower than heathenism, for the heathens never *eat* their God. These men are sanctimonious and exceedingly devoted to the poor. Yes, and they are most zealous in attending their churches, and in attending to their monstrous developments. This is of the same character as that described with reference to Korah. But the only sense in which these men should preach is when they become really sons of God, redeemed Christians, because that is the only sense in which they will be received ; but all this false doctrine of the Oxford School denies that all Christians are priests, and infringes and overthrows the real work of Christ, and substitutes this continual sacrifice, which is a sin. So that no wonder Jude says, " Woe unto them ! for they have gone in the way of Cain, and run greedily after the error of Balaam for reward, and perished in the gainsaying of Korah."

Then note the tremendous words that follow : " These are spots in your love-feasts." Think of it. There were such men at that time in the church. Therefore we ought never to be surprised at anything evil that may break out in the world ; the only thing is for believers to fight the good fight of faith. There is another rendering—" Hidden rocks in your love-feasts, feasting together, fearlessly pasturing themselves ; clouds " they are, and it should be noted they are " without water," without the real work of the Spirit of God, the rich refreshment of it—" carried along by winds." As I said before, I will not deny that God may use any person in a solemn way which is thought to be a good deal of honour in the priesthood, but it is deadly work for themselves who preach. " Autumnal trees without fruit, twice dead, rooted up ; raging waves of the sea foaming out their own shames : wandering stars for whom hath been reserved the gloom of darkness for ever."

May God preserve His saints, and may we by watchfulness and prayer be carried safely through such dangers as these.

VERSES 14, 15

" AND Enoch, seventh from Adam, prophesied also
as to these, saying, Behold, [the] Lord came amid
His holy myriads, to execute judgment against all,
and to convict all the ungodly [of them] of all their
works of ungodliness which they ungodlily wrought,
and of all the hard things which ungodly sinners
spoke against him " (vers. 14, 15).

This is a remarkable utterance, for which we can
only account as being in the power of the Holy
Ghost.

There is a traditional book of Enoch in the
Ethiopic language, which appears to have been
known in a Greek form now long lost. We have not
got the Greek, but learned men have endeavoured
with all possible zeal to try and make out that Jude
quotes from this uninspired book ; for the book is
evidently one of Jewish tradition, and from internal
evidence it would seem that it was written after
the destruction of Jerusalem. But there is another
thing that appears, I think, to anyone that reads
it with, not merely learning, but with spiritual
understanding, which is, that it differs essentially
in this very verse, supposed by some to be quoted
from it, from what Jude has here given us by the
Spirit of God.

But how was Jude enabled to quote the words of
Enoch, who was taken up to heaven before the
flood—and nothing can be plainer than that he

does give it as Enoch's words ? " Enoch prophesied,"
he says. Well, I think that to us who know the
power of the Spirit of God there is no real difficulty
in the matter. It is all the same to Him to record
what took place three thousand years ago as it
would be to record what took place at the time the
apostles lived. It may be a little more difficult to
those who doubt this power, if they do ; but we
are the last who ought to do so.

The fact is, that no tradition has any value
beyond man, but a prophecy necessarily, if it is a
true one, comes from God. We have no intimation
that it was conveyed in any written form, and it
was quite possible for the Holy Ghost to have given
it again to Jude. I do not at all venture to say that
it was so ; we really do not know, but we do know,
however Jude got it, that it is divine. We know
that it is given with absolute certainty, and that it
possesses God's authority.

There is a peculiarity when it says, " Enoch also,
the seventh from Adam." People have made somewhat of that because they do not understand it.
But it is very simple. There was more than one
Enoch.

There was an Enoch before this one—an Enoch
the son of Cain. I do not see any ground to imagine
something peculiar and mystical in this. At any
rate, if there be such, I confess I do not know what
it is. But I do know that there is a plain and
sufficient sense to distinguish this Enoch, and to

explain how he could prophesy. We should not
look for prophecy in a son of Cain. But that Enoch
taken up to heaven in a most remarkable way—
more so, in some respects, than the case of any
other man ; more so than Elijah, though that was a
miracle of similar import and character—that Enoch
should be the medium of prophecy we can quite
understand, for he walked with God, and was not.
It was not that he died, but " he was not," because
he was taken up to God ; yet before he left the
world, he prophesied. We can hardly doubt that
he prophesied about the people of his own day.
Prophecy always takes its start from what is
actually present, and has a hold in the consciences
of those then living. The object was to warn of the
terrible consequences of evil that was persisted in,
and how the evil then appearing would assuredly
be judged of God in due time. But the Spirit of
God also launches out to the end from the beginning.
This is the common character of all prophecy. We
find it throughout all the prophets at any rate.
I do not, of course, say that it was always the case
where the prediction was about something of a
merely present nature, but it was so in the cases of
those moral pictures which are not bound to any
particular time or person. We can quite understand
these being made the vehicle for the Spirit of God
to look on to the time of judgment when it would
not be providential action of the Lord, such as the
flood, for instance, but—much more than any

acting after that figurative manner—His real personal coming in judgment.

Now, in that Ethiopic book which I have seen, and of which I have the text and English translation by the late Archbishop Laurence, as well as a French version of the work by a very learned Romanist (perhaps a more excellent scholar than the Archbishop I have named, at any rate one more familiar with Oriental languages)—they both agree in what is totally different from what we have here ; and what makes it more remarkable is, they agree in asserting an error which is almost universal now in Christendom.

You are aware that the general view of all Christians who derive their thoughts from traditions, creeds, or articles of faith, is that everyone will be judged alike ; and this view falls in quite with the natural thought, particularly of the natural man. It seems to them a very offensive thing that those who are really sinners like themselves, but are believers unlike themselves, should not be judged. It seems, to them, since they think very little of believing, a very hard and unrighteous thing that believers should be exempted from a judgment to which others are fast hastening.

But why ? Our Lord puts it in the clearest possible manner in John v. He there describes Himself in two different lights—one as Son of God, the other as Son of man. As Son of God He gives life. And who are they who get life ? Does He not

tell us that he " that believes on Him hath life
eternal " ? It is one of those remarkable, short and
pithy statements of the Gospel of John. In one
form or another it runs through the entire Gospel,
I might almost say from the first chapter, though
we may not have the literal words, but the same
fundamental, substantial sense. And it goes on all
through this Gospel, to chapter xx. certainly, if not
to xxi. And the same great truth re-appears in his
First Epistle ; that life belongs to him that believes
on the Lord Jesus. Just as surely as we inherit
death naturally from Adam, so now there is another
man who is also God, and being God as well as Man,
He has entirely set aside for us the judgment of our
sins by bearing it Himself. But that is not all. He
gives us this new life which is proper to Himself
that we might be able to bear fruit for God now.
There must be a good life to bear good fruit. And
there is no good life to bear fruit that God counts
good except Christ's life, and all that are of faith
have received that life—every Old Testament saint,
as really as a New Testament saint. They had
faith, they had life, they testified for God. Their
ways were holy, which they could not have been
had they not a life to produce this holiness ; and so
it is now.

Well, accordingly, those that believe on Him,
the Son of God, receive life. If I reject His divine
glory, that is, that He is the Son of God in this high
and full sense, then I have not life ; because He

only gives it to those that believe. But do those
who remain in unbelief therefore escape ? No, He
is Son of man ; and this is just where their want of
faith broke down. They could see that He was a
man, and as they had no faith to see anything deeper,
they only regarded Him as Son of man. In this
very character the Lord will judge them. He will
judge them as the Man Whom they despised. They
will behold Him as the Man of everlasting glory.
Not merely a divine person, but a Man ; and in
that very quality—as Son of man—He will judge
them.

Now, there would be no sense in, or reason for,
judging the believer, even if it were not said by our
Lord that the believer shall not come into judgment.
Because, what would he come into judgment for ?
If any go into judgment, it is a reality. It must be
so if God were to enter into judgment with even
believers. Were they never guilty of sins ? And if
these sins come into judgment, they cannot escape
punishment ; and if they are judged, they are lost.
But if Christ has borne their sins, where would be
the object or wisdom of putting them on their trial
after they are acquitted and justified ? And we are
justified now by faith. All believers are. Every
Christian is. It is not a question of peculiar views.
I hate peculiar views. Peculiar views are the errors
of men. It would be a most shameful thing to
count God's truth to be " peculiar views." The
only thing a Christian should care for is God's

truth. It is only the language of an enemy to count
that " peculiar views." If there *are* those that try
to blacken it and call it peculiar views their blood
must be on their own heads. The language is the
language of an adversary. We have nothing to do
with running after new views or innovations of any
kind, and God forbid that we should care for one
single thing that is an innovation. I call an
innovation anything that is a departure from God's
word.

It is not the antiquity of sixteen or seventeen
centuries, but we go to the very beginning, to the
apostles, and to the Lord Himself ; and there is the
source from which we may draw and know for
ourselves immediately, just as truly as if we had the
apostles here before us. The apostles were certainly
not more inspired when they spoke and preached
than when they wrote ; but it was what they wrote
that was made to convey down the stream of ages
divine truth with the utmost possible certainty.
There is a great advantage in having what is written.
You can come and come again. Even if you
listened to an apostle, or to the Lord, you might
forget. You might slip away from His words and
put in some of your own. There is nothing more
common than this every day, even with very
accurate people ; they do not carry absolutely
every word. It is too serious a thing not to have the
word of God, and it is of the utmost importance that
we have it written. What we want is the truth

first-hand—from the people inspired to give it—
and this is just what we have. And the simplest
man is responsible to weigh and consider it.

It may be said he is a weak soul. Well, we are
all too apt to think too much of ourselves. Especially,
if men have a little ability, they are apt to over-
estimate what they have. There is nothing more
common than this, and nothing more dangerous.
Whereas, if a man is really a weak soul and does not
think much about himself there is far more readiness
to learn ; unless he is an obstinate man, who, even
though he knows but very little, thinks a deal of
himself. There is nothing so dangerous as that,
especially when such a one lifts himself up against
the word of God. When a man is brought to God,
he is made nothing of in his own eyes. Would to
God we always stayed there, with the sense of our
own nothingness ! Would to God that it did not
evaporate by our getting peace ! There is always a
danger of a person forgetting that there was a time
when he counted nothing that he thought, said, or
felt, was worth thinking about. We are meant to
keep that humility always. The best and truest
form of real humility is the sense of the presence of
God and of the infinite value of the word of God.
There is nothing so humble as bowing to God's
authority, there is nothing so humble as obedience—
obeying God. And at the same time, nothing gives
greater courage, nothing gives greater confidence,
nothing gives greater firmness ; and this humility

is exactly what we want—to be nothing in our own
eyes, and to have perfect confidence in God's word.
And faith should produce this in every believer.

Not only, then, does the Lord lay down that the
believer, " comes not into judgment," but He
declares what the end will be. Not that there will
be only one resurrection. Were there but one
resurrection, it might be no wonder that there will
be only one judgment ; but to confirm the fact
that there will be no judgment of the believer—no
sitting in judgment on him to decide his lot for
eternity—there are two resurrections spoken of in
that very same passage in the fifth chapter of John ;
and I would commend that chapter to anyone who
has not duly weighed it. There it is shown that there
will be a " resurrection of life " for those that have
life for their souls already ; there will be a " resurrection of judgment " for those that have not life but
sins, and not merely sins but unbelief, the refusal
of that life. They rejected the Son of God ! For
them there is judgment, and for them there is a
special resurrection at the close of all. For those that
have life now, in the Son, there is " the first resurrection," a life-resurrection. Other saints, too, will
share in this, for though not at the same moment,
their resurrection, nevertheless, will have this
character. All that are Christ's who are in their
graves when the Lord comes will rise together, and
the living that are on the earth at that time will
be changed, while others who die afterwards will

follow, as we learn from the book of Revelation, which is my reason for guarding the statement. They all have a resurrection of life, except those that do not die, and will be brought into the change without resurrection ; but their change will be equivalent to resurrection, so that it may be all called, in a certain way, a " resurrection of life."

But there is also a " resurrection of judgment " for all those that despise Christ, for all that are sinners against God, for all who have refused the Saviour, from the beginning of the world up to that time ; and the resurrection of judgment is at the end of all time. Not so the resurrection of life ; and the reason why it is not is this—that those who rise in the resurrection of life rise to reign with Christ, before the winding up of all things. The wind up of all will be after all the ages have run their course, so that the last sinner may be included in that awful resurrection—" the resurrection of judgment." We need not call it a " resurrection of damnation," because the word used is distinct from that. In effect it comes to that, but it is not the force of the word. It is always better to stand to the exact word of God, even if we do not understand it. We owe it honour and reverence, whether we understand it or not. His word must be right, it must be wise and the best, the only one that is really good and reliable absolutely.

This may seem a long preamble, but it is necessary,

perhaps, to make the force plain of what I am going
to remark here.

In the spurious book of Enoch, from which the
learned people maintain that Jude quoted, the
doctrine taught is that the Lord " comes with ten
thousands of His saints to execute judgment upon
them." There you see is the error that betrays the
devil in the forger, for from this very verse, I do
not in the least doubt that that document has been
forged. It has every mark of having been written,
subsequent to the destruction of Jerusalem, by a
Jew who still buoyed himself up with the hope that
God would stand by the Jews.

And so He will in the end, but in a way totally
different from what he, the writer, supposed. For
there is no true acknowledgment of Christ. He is
simply acknowledged as the Messiah from a Jewish
point of view, but there never will be deliverance
for the Jew in looking for the Messiah according to
their thoughts. It is the Messiah of God, the
Anointed of Jehovah, the true Messiah that came,
and they rejected Him. But when He comes to
deliver them by and by they will be brought to
say, " Blessed is He that cometh in the name of the
Lord." They will then give up all their unbelief,
they will welcome Him, and He will come and
deliver them, and He will save them out of all that
strait of trouble in which they will then be.

But He will not judge His own people. He was
judged for them, He bore their judgment on the

tree, and He will never judge them. Nor is there one word in the Bible—Old or New Testament—that insinuates in the most distant manner that the Lord will inflict judgment on His own people. That He will judge His people is a common thing in the Old Testament. But that will be, as a King, the judgment of their difficulties, their disorders if there should be any ; and He will also vindicate them from their enemies. It is in this sense that He will judge His people.

Moreover, God carries on a moral judgment now in respect to His children. " If ye call on the Father, Who without respect of persons judgeth according to every man's work, pass the time of your sojourning [here] in fear." This is still going on. The Lord dealt with the Corinthians in this way. When they were in such a bad state and profaned the table of the Lord, coming boldly and taking the bread and the wine as if they had been in a good state, the Lord laid His hand on them—some were sick, some fell asleep—were removed by death. All this was a temporal judgment. It is what the Lord does now, and this judgment is for our good and profit.

We see the same thing in a family. It is the judgment that a father carries on in his family, or any person charged with the care of youths put under him—young persons of either sex. Well, there is a judgment for their good. This is a totally different thing from what is called in John v. a " coming into

judgment." It is even a different word employed—a
different form of the word. From Psalm cxliii. it is
evident that the Old Testament saints knew better
than that. At any rate, the Spirit of God gave
them better knowledge, for there it says, " Enter
not into judgment with Thy servant : for in Thy
sight shall no man living be justified." If God
were to enter into judgment with the believer it
would be all over with him, because even the
believer himself would be bound to say, I do not
deserve to be saved. And if God were to look at all
the faults in a believer's life He might say, if that
is what I have to look at, I have no reason to save
you, you do not deserve it. But the ground of a
believer's salvation is not that he deserves it, but
that Christ deserves it for us. Christ has completely
met all God's nature, and, further than that, He
has borne all our sins and iniquities in His own body
on the tree. God will not judge them again as if
they had not been sufficiently borne, as if the
judgment at the cross were not an adequate one.
God will never say that about what Christ endured,
and this is just what faith lays hold of. Therefore,
the uniform doctrine of the Bible—of both Old and
New Testament—is this, that believers are not to
come into that future judgment which the Lord
will execute at the close of all things ; but
because we now have life, and are God's children,
He watches over and cares for us, and carries
on a moral judgment ; and besides this, the

Lord Jesus carries on now a judgment of the church.

We find, besides the Father judging individually His children, that the Lord Jesus takes up the things that pertain to His name among those that are assembled together. He is Head of the church, and He has a watchful eye that the things that are done under His holy name should be real, should not be hypocritical, that His name should not be profaned. If our ways are unreal, and we go on badly, He deals with us in the way of discipline, and for the very reason " that we should not be condemned with the world." There you have the reason. If He did not do so, you might raise a question as to whether they would be lost.

Now then, the author of this spurious Book of Enoch understood not a word of all this. He was not a believer. He was a false man ; he would never have forged if he had not been. He was a forger of the worst kind. No forgery is so bad as that which pretends to give us the word of God. It is very bad to be deceitful in anything, but if deceit is carried on in the things of God there is none that is worse in its consequences, there is none that more distinctly dishonours God. And that is the case here.

" Behold, the Lord cometh with ten thousands of His saints, to———" what does scripture say ? to " execute judgment upon all." This is not the saints. The " all " are totally distinct from the saints. The saints had been caught up, and now come with

Him Who executes the judgment on all the sinners to be found in that day. " To execute judgment upon all, and to convince all "—to make it perfectly plain who are meant—all " that are ungodly among them." There it is, to obviate any argument, for there are people who are not great in the truth who are always ready for an argument ! Here we see it is " to execute judgment upon all, and to convince all that are ungodly among them " (that is, these " all ") " of all their ungodly deeds which they have ungodlily committed." And not only ungodly deeds ; there is another thing that the Spirit of God attaches great importance to—" hard words which ungodly sinners spoke against Him," words that gainsay God's mind, words that say the thing that is false of God. Job's friends did that. Job himself bowed to God. He had not many words, he made a confession of his folly, he said the thing that was right. But his friends had not spoken the thing that was right of the Lord. I do not think that the Lord was putting the stamp of His approval in the same way on *all* that Job said. He often spoke haughtily, and unhappily about God, and fretted about himself, but the Lord does not refer to that. Job broke down and confessed his nothingness. His friends did not break down. Job did, and, in consequence, Job was restored, and had to pray for those, his friends, who were not as yet restored.

But here it is plain that ungodly words are just

as bad in their own way as ungodly deeds. Sometimes an ungodly word does more harm than an ungodly deed. For instance, an ungodly deed might be an act of unrighteousness in a man, but an ungodly word might be a slurring of Christ. This is worse, and particularly if people receive it. People are quite ready to cry out against an ungodly deed. Even worldly men can very well judge ungodly deeds, and the same people would be deceived by hard and ungodly words against the Lord and His grace and truth.

In this Book of Enoch to which I have referred there is not a word about the " hard speeches." This shows that the author was simply a natural man ; a man who, no doubt, had this phrase before him, but he did not understand it. He evidently did not understand either about the saint or about the sinner. He did not understand about the saints, because he made them objects of judgment as well as the ungodly. It is just like the theologians now. They do not believe what I am now saying. But there is one word, in leaving that subject, that I wish to add. " We shall all be manifested before the judgment seat of Christ." Everything, good or bad, will come out, for the believer as well as for the unbeliever. But that is a very different thing from judgment. This is not called judgment, but " manifestation," which is not the same thing as judgment. Manifestation of all our ways will be a very good thing for us. How apt we are to

overrate ourselves ! There may be something that
we perhaps flattered ourselves about while we were
here alive, and we never saw how foolish we were
till risen from the dead and standing before the
judgment seat of Christ.   There it will all be
manifested.   Where we thought that we were wise
we shall see that we were very foolish.   And so in
everything where we may have allowed ourselves a
little latitude and tried to excuse ourselves, we shall
there be obliged to acknowledge it as all wrong.
This is for our good.   It is a blessing to do it in this
life, but it will be all the fullest and richest blessing
there.   All will be out then.   Then we shall know
even as also we are known.   We shall have no
thought different from God's about a single thing
in all our lives.   But this is not judgment.   Judgment
is where a person stands to be tried, and to be
convicted of his guilt.   This will be the case with
everyone who has not been justified by the Lord
Jesus Christ and His incomparable work on the
cross.

But there is a second point where this forger
could not copy the text before him aright.   He only
speaks of " ungodly *deeds*."   Hard, ungodlily
spoken " words " to him did not seem of very much
account, so he left out the ungodly " words."   The
first part seemed the only right thing to him.
Consequently, he mutilated the scripture.   He could
not even copy it truly, and thus he has given us a
false version of it.

In other words, Jude never got his prophecy of
Enoch from a mere tradition, or from this book at
all. He got it from God. How, I do not pretend to
say. But he did.

VERSES 16–19

" THESE are murmurers, complainers, walking after
their lusts, and their mouth speaketh swelling
things, admiring persons for the sake of profit. But
ye, beloved, remember ye the words that were
spoken before by the apostles of our Lord Jesus
Christ, that they said to you, In [the] end of the
time shall be mockers walking after their own lusts
of ungodliness.   These are they that make
separations, natural (or, soulish), not having [the]
Spirit " (vers. 16–19).

" These are murmurers." Murmuring is a more
serious sin than many think. It could not but be
that among Christians there are many things that
do not go according to what we like. Suppose it
to be even a man of sound wisdom ; but if people
are not very well founded they are always apt to
be disappointed at something in him. It is natural
for people to begin to murmur. The Israelites were
constantly at that kind of work.

Now, he says, " There are murmurers," and he
adds, " complainers "—not content with their lot
(the strict literal meaning of the word). They are
persons who like to be something more and greater

than they are, than God ever called them to be.
They want to be somebody.

" These are murmurers, complainers " ; and what
is the cause of that ? " Walking after their own
lusts." Lust is not to be supposed to be merely
gross lusts. There are refined lusts—vanity, pride,
ambition ; what are all these but lusts ? They are
all lusts. The lusts of the devil. These are not
the same kind of lusts as the lusts of the flesh.
Satan was lifted up with pride, and we are warned
against falling into the fault or " condemnation "
of the devil. It appears that the things mentioned
in this verse are very much the same thing : " their
mouth speaketh great swelling words, having men's
persons in admiration because of advantage."
They are fond of having a party, particularly if
they can number some rich among the party,
" because of advantage."

What I particularly draw your attention to is
this. Enoch prophesied of these. I do not know
anything more striking than that. There are the
same persons now as in Enoch's day. There can
be no doubt that these people lived in the time of
Enoch. But Jude carried us on to the coming of
the Lord. The people who are on the earth when
the Lord comes will be the same kind in their
wickedness as in the days of Enoch and of Jude.
Evil, you see, goes on. Evil retains its own terrible
character—malignancy and rebellion against God,
and all self-sufficiency, and all the terrible things

that are so entirely opposed to Christ. Enoch prophesied of these and of the judgment coming upon them.

" But ye, beloved, remember ye "—to confirm this—" the words that were spoken before by the apostles of our Lord Jesus Christ, how that they told you that there should be mockers in the last time, who should walk after their own ungodly lusts " (vers. 17, 18).

Well, we have at least two of these apostles. Surely, that is quite enough. Very likely the other apostles taught the very same things by word of mouth. But we have this warning about these characters, written down by two besides Jude ; one the apostle Paul, the other Peter in both his Epistles. In his First, Peter says that the time is coming when judgment must begin at the house of God, and judgment on just this kind of ungodliness then working up ; but in his Second Epistle there is a deal more. And I think that Jude goes still further, and that his Epistle was written after Second Peter, and for this reason, that there is an advance of evil. Peter speaks of unrighteous men, Jude speaks of men that once seemed to have the truth, and through their bad life, bad ways, pride, vanity, or whatever it was, they lost it. That is quite a common thing. By common, I do not mean that any very great numbers break off in this way, but that it is a sin which every now and then breaks out. Why, even since " Brethren " began there have been the most terrible cases of people giving up all the truth. The greatest infidel of modern days was one of the early "brethren." He was a very clever man, and gave up his fellowship at Balliol to go to the Eastern world, among Arabs and Persians and the like, with the gospel. He seemed to be devoted to the Lord. But even on his way out he betrayed that he was not a true believer at all. How! By doubting about the full proper Deity of the Lord Jesus ; and when he came back brethren enquired into it. There had been whispers of it before his return, but then he was out of the way, so that till his return it was not possible to deal with him fairly, or to examine him fully, not merely whispers. When he came back he was seen and written to, and his words were the words of an unbeliever ; he was therefore refused any place in our fellowship. After this, he went among the dissenters, who welcomed him most heartily, and he preached in their chapels and was most acceptable among them, particularly as he ran down the "brethren" pretty hotly. At this time, he still appeared to be pious in his outward ways and manner, and still read the Bible. But he gradually gave up everything and gave an account of it in a book which he wrote bearing a very anomalous title indeed, for it would appear that he really never had faith. He was a man who was very impressionable, and he easily took the colour of those with whom he was. He valued and was charmed with the sound of the truth, and thought he had it, but I am afraid he never had. So he lived, and so, I fear, he died. There have been others of no such prominence who have had a similar end ; not so marked, perhaps, but as sad. Some had once been in fellowship, and seemed to be very honoured persons for a time, before they were really known. And this kind of thing falls in with what we have here.

There were such persons among them ; and not merely the teachers. Peter speaks about teachers, but Jude looks at them more widely ; they are evidently responsible even though they are not teachers. If others dishonour the Lord who are not teachers, they are responsible. There is this character in Jude : they are apostate from the truth, and have not gone out of fellowship yet. That is the very thing he says. There they are, although it is likely that no one but Jude who saw these persons could speak of them ; and Peter saw them where he was. They appeared fair enough just as there were many such at the time when the person referred to was in fellowship. Many would not believe a word of it. They thought he was a very good man, and that it was a scandal to speak hardly about him. They never could see till the thing came out thoroughly. We are not all " eyes " in the body. We may have an important place. The hand or the foot can do a work that the eye cannot, and there are those who can see far before

others ; and it is important for people to make use
of those who have proved their special competence.
Otherwise we are apt to get wrong.

It is an immense thing to say that we have not
only teachers now and preachers to spread the
truth in spite of their weakness and their liability
to err, but we have also those that were kept from
error in what they have written, absolutely kept
from error ; and these are here brought before us as
the apostles of our Lord Jesus Christ. They were
men of like passions as we are ourselves, but the
peculiarity in the case of those apostles and prophets
is, that in the midst of their weakness they were
preserved—It was not, it is true, like Christ, absolute
perfection—but there was the perfect preservation
from error in what they wrote. And it was all the
more remarkable that this was in one generation
only. It was not like the succession that there
was in the old dispensation of God. There we have
prophets raised up at all times, wherever they
were needed ; but the great peculiarity for the
church and for the Christian is that we have not
merely words that were perfect for their purpose,
and words that were given faithfully by God in the
midst of all the errors of Israel, but now we have a
perfect revelation in all respects, by men themselves
imperfect, but nevertheless kept and empowered by
the Holy Ghost to say the truth without error
whatever.

Now, there are two things in the words of the

apostles ; the first is the mind of God for the glory
of Christ ; and this we have in all the books of the
New Testament. But in the midst of these words,
and more particularly in the latter times of giving
these words we have the most solemn warnings that
are given in any part of the Bible. It was not at all
that all these characters of evil came out so that
the Christian could discern them, but they came out
sufficiently for the apostles to discern them.

Thus we have our lessons for practical guidance
in the words of the apostles. They are the persons
through whom we have received the full truth of
God. There was not an error that ever crept into
the church but is provided for here. There is not a
good thing that God had to reveal but what is
revealed here.

For we are not meant to be inventors, we are not
meant to make discoveries, like the men of science.
The reason why there are inventions in the arts,
and discoveries in science, is, because all is imperfect.
But perfection is what marks the word of God—not
merely relative perfection, relative to the state of
Israel at different times, but—absolute perfection.
What brought in absolute perfection ? Christ.
There is the key to all that is blessed, to all that is
most blessed. There is what explains what is
most of all peculiar. It was according to Christ that
all the truth should be brought out, unstinted, and
perfectly providing for everything that might be
through the ages that follow down to the present

time. And this in order that we might never have
to look outside scripture for the proof of any error,
and this also for the provision of everything good.
All is in the word ; this word that we have got.
The Old Testament is full of value, but, nevertheless,
it is only general. Our special instructions are in
the New Testament, for we can easily understand
that there was no such thing as a Christian in Old
Testament times. They were believers, but not
Christians. A Christian is a man who is not merely
looking for the promises, but who has the promises—
accomplished in Christ. Well, of course, the Old
Testament saints had not got this, and the church
was an absolutely new thing. It was not merely
promises accomplished, but the mystery revealed :
the mystery that was hid in God up to that time.
There was no revelation of it in the Old Testament
whatever. Now it is revealed, and it is given to us.
And how ? By these perfect writings of the New
Testament, that left nothing to desire, nothing for
faith to desire ; plenty for unbelief to add, still
more for unbelief to depart from ; but nothing for
faith to desire. We have all here, and it is only for
our faith to discern it, and to practise it.

Now for this reason all came out in one generation.
John, the very last of all, was the one that saw the
Lord from the beginning. He was, not only one of
the apostles, but, one of the first two that ever
followed the Lord Jesus and entered into living
relationship with Him here below. And he was

kept here, beyond others, in the wisdom of God. But we have another, also, of those who were eminently favoured, and were conspicuously used. Although Jude wrote a short Epistle, what a great deal there is in it !

Now, turning to what we have already touched upon—" But ye, beloved, remember ye the words which were spoken before by the apostles of our Lord Jesus Christ ; that they said to you, In [the] end of the time shall be mockers walking after their own lusts of ungodliness " ; that there should be, not merely unrighteous men, or lawless men, but, one of the worst features of evil, " mockers." Why, in the Old Testament, when it was only a question of children that could not resist giving way to their humour—I may call it very bad humour, and very bad manners—but still they mocked the old prophet, they mocked Elisha. And even he, the man of grace, was no doubt led of God to call forth the bears that tore them all.

Here we find that it is not little children in their folly (for we know that " foolishness is bound in the heart of a child "), but the case of men who claimed wisdom ; and the way they showed it was by " mocking " ! " Mockers in the last time, who should walk after their own ungodly lusts "—their own lusts of ungodly things. It is rather stronger. Their lust was after ungodliness. This is what characterised their lust. It is not a mere vague term ; it is a very succinct term—" lusts of ungodliness." Now this is an awful thing. And resulting from what ? I will not say it results from Christianity, from the truth. God forbid. But it resulted from the fact that they were there, and that their hearts got tired of it, and they became the enemies of it. There is nothing more blessed than a Christian man walking in simplicity. There is nothing more awful than a Christian man who casts off Christianity, and who becomes a mocker after the lusts of his own ungodliness. This is what is described here, and what the writer prepares us for. No one could have believed that in early days.

These mockers once looked fair. They once spoke fairly. They were received, they were baptised ; they remembered the Lord Jesus, taking part in the assembly, no doubt. They may have been preachers, very likely ; but here it was evident they were given up to their own lusts of ungodliness and they were mockers ; accordingly, they therefore turned with the greatest spite and hatred upon that truth that once separated them from the world. They were professedly believers, but it is evident they were in reality the emissaries of Satan. And the Epistles (some of the last in the Bible), as well as the apostles of our Lord, laid down this : that these mockers were to come in the last time. The last time was therefore to be a peculiarly evil time, and it is a very solemn thing that we are in that time most fully now. I do not say that it may not be lengthened—that is entirely a question of the

will of God. The lengthening of evil may be just
as much as the lengthening of tranquillity. There is
the tranquillity for one, and it may end in greater
departure than ever, or it may be the means of
repentance, and extrication from these toils of the
enemy.

But here at any rate he declares, " These are
they who separate themselves, sensual, having not
the Spirit " (ver. 19).   It is important to understand
this verse, for there are various kinds of separations
mentioned in the New Testament.   Sometimes, it is
separation within ;   sometimes, it is separation
without ;   sometimes, it takes the character of
parties as yet joined with the rest in outward
observances, but their spirit alienated.   Those are
the persons the apostle refers to in Romans xvi. :
persons " which cause divisions and stumbling-
blocks, contrary to the doctrine which ye have
learned " (ver. 17).   That doctrine was that we
should walk, not only outwardly together but,
inwardly, with real love.   It is true it may not
always be approving of what each may do and say,
but with earnest desire that things might go well,
and that those even who are in any way caught by
the enemy might be delivered.

Now, the persons in Romans xvi. were not to be
" put away," but avoided ; and the object of that
avoiding was to make them feel and reflect upon
what they were about.   Suppose they were preachers
or teachers, avoiding such would be not to invite

them, or if they invited themselves, not to accept
their offer. Of course, you can understand that
they would not like it, unless they were really
broken in spirit. In this case all would terminate
happily, but if they were bent on doing their own
will they ought to be avoided as the apostle says,
and if they do not like this avoiding, and grow
bitter under it, the effect would be that they would
make a division " without " if they could, instead
of " within." They would " go out " themselves,
and try and lead away others.

There are these kinds of spirits. First, they have
an alienated mind within, and are self-seeking ; and
because this is blamed by all that have the good
of the saints at heart, and the glory of the Lord
before them, they resent it strongly, and, instead of
breaking down and judging themselves, they
become worse, and then it is not a division " within,"
but " without," that they make. The former is
called a schism, the latter a heresy. For I particularly
press it on every one here who may not have
observed it—that " heresy " in scripture does not
mean bad doctrine at all. There may be bad
doctrine, of course, along with it ; but this is
rather heterodoxy—strange doctrine. There are
proper terms for all forms of evil : falsehood, deceit,
blasphemy and the like. But heresy means the self-
will that does not care for the fellowship of the
assembly in the least, and is so bent on its own
object that it goes outside. This is what is called

heresy. Now that is what the apostle means in
1 Cor. xi. He says, " There are divisions (or,
schisms) among you. For there must be also heresies
(or, sects) among you, that they which are approved
may be made manifest among you " (vers. 18, 19).

But there is no " must be " in reference to
heterodoxy. People might remain, and like to
remain, with their heterodoxy, but heresy does not
mean bad doctrine, although this might go along
with it. It means that people might get too hot
in their zeal, and, being reproved for their party
spirit, they refuse to stand it any longer, and they
get away. They break loose from fellowship and
form some new thing which has not the sanction of
the word of God. That is what, in scripture,
is called heresy. The doctrine might be sound
enough in a general way. There might be no
blasphemies, nor heterodoxy, strictly speaking, but
there is the heart entirely wrong and seeking its
own things instead of the things of Jesus Christ.

So in the verse before us, " These be they who
separate themselves " means those that separate
themselves " within," not " without," at all. This
is very evident from the early part of this Epistle :
" For there are certain men crept in unawares, who
were before of old ordained to this condemnation,
ungodly men, turning the grace of our God into
lasciviousness, and denying the only Lord God,
and our Lord Jesus Christ " (ver. 4). Certain men
crept in. They are the same people that Jude is

talking about all through. Unawares, they had
" crept in," not " gone out." Now this is what
gives the true force of the words—" those that
separate themselves." We can easily understand it
if we bear in mind the Pharisees. The Pharisees
never separated themselves from Israel, but the
very name of a Pharisee means " a separatist."
They were separatists within Israel. These were
separatists within the church, and in both cases it
was not going out, but it was making a party of
pride and self-righteousness within. And who are
they ? Ungodly men ; these were the men that
were proud of themselves ; these men who had these
wicked lusts. They were the persons who assumed
to be pre-eminently faithful ; and, I believe, you
will generally find that it is so, that, when persons
are given up to delusion, they always have a very
high opinion of themselves. No matter how violent
they may be, no matter how evil in their spirit,
they claim to be more particularly faithful, and
they have no measure in their denunciation of every
one that stands in their way. This is exactly the
class here described.

" These be they who separate themselves." And
what sort of men were they ? " Sensual." The word
" sensual " is important to understand. Every man
has got a soul, converted or not. Now, when we
believe, we receive a nature that we never had
before ; we receive life in Christ. These men here
described had nothing but their natural soul. They

had not received life in Christ. They were merely
" natural " men. " Sensual," in our language, is
very often taken to mean people who are abandoned
to immoral ways. These people may have been so,
but it is not the meaning of the word. The meaning
of the word is that they were just simply " natural "
men. It is the same word which, in 1 Cor. ii. 14,
is translated " natural man," and contrasted with the
" spiritual man." So he adds here, " not having
the Spirit."

Now, having not the Spirit is to lack the great
privilege of a Christian. This is the great difference
between a believer now resting on redemption, and
an Old Testament believer. They were waiting for
the Spirit in the days of the Messiah. Although the
Messiah is rejected, the Holy Ghost has been poured
down on us, but not on those that are still waiting
for the Messiah. The Jews are still waiting, and
have not the Spirit. These men, although they had
taken their place in the church, had not the Spirit.
They were natural men. We are therefore given this
further development of the terrible evil that had
come in even then, although the great mass of the
saints, you may be sure, very little understood it,
very little perceived it ; and therefore it was of the
greatest moment that the apostles should. And
that there should be inspired men, or, at any rate,
inspired instruction given upon what people otherwise
would not have been in the least prepared for, and
would have counted it a very fierce and terrible

picture without any good ground for it ; they would
think it was making the worst of everything instead
of the best.   But the Spirit of God does give the
truth just as it is.

VERSES 20, 21

WELL, now we come to a very comforting word.
" But ye, beloved, building up yourselves on your
most holy faith, praying in [the] Holy Spirit, keep
yourselves in [the] love of God, awaiting the mercy
of our Lord Jesus Christ unto life eternal " (vers.
20, 21).

So then we are not to be cast down, we are not
to be disheartened, even by these terrible pictures
of evil.   They are revealed in order that we should
not be deceived, that we may really know what the
actual state of Christianity is before the eye of God,
instead of yielding to false expectations and wrong
and imperfect judgments of our own.   But even in
the face of all that, there is this call to these beloved
saints to build up themselves on their most holy
faith.   This is very carefully worded.   There is
nothing at all said in this Epistle about leaders, or
guides, or rulers, or preachers, or teachers either.
In a general way, as far as there were any, they
have a very bad character, not of course that all
who preached or taught were so, but that there
were many of this class that were so especially.
The saints themselves are here exhorted directly.

They are not to give up their privileges, or to
imagine, that because it is a day of such abounding
evil, they are not to be very happy. They are
comforted with this ; that the blessing is perfectly
open to them, and they are called to have more
faith than ever. There is no time when faith shines
brighter than in the dark day, and there is no time
when love is more evidently discerned than when
there are not many to love, not many that do love,
but where there is the reign of selfishness and
indifference, and people care for other objects, and
put them before that which is imperishable.

" But ye, beloved, building up yourselves on your
most holy faith." This is the only place in all the
New Testament where faith is called our " most holy
faith." It might have been thought that when
things are so evidently wrong we must not be too
stringent, that we must not be too exacting, that
we must not look for such care as on the day of Pentecost. Why, so far from that being so, we require more
care. And instead of its being now called merely
the holy faith, or precious faith, Jude calls it,
" your most holy faith." The saints, in short, are
encouraged to cleave to the truth in all its sanctifying
power. We cannot think too much of " the faith of
God's elect." I am not speaking now of faith
looked at in the saint, but of " the faith " looked
at in itself. It is the thing that we believe, which
is the meaning of it here. It is not crying up
individuals, but what these individuals receive from

God. That is what he calls it—" the faith." There
is a great difference between faith and " the faith."
Here it is " the faith." Faith is a quality of you,
and me, and every believer. But that is not the
sense here, which is, " the faith once delivered to
the saints," as he says in this very Epistle.

Well, thus you must look at it. When it came,
you may say, It came down from God out of heaven,
revealed through the apostles—Christ Himself of
course in particular. There, was " the faith " :
what we are called to believe ; that which separated
us to God from everything here below. So here,
we have the same faith, only—it is not now said,
" once for all delivered to the saints," although this
remains true. Here it is called " most holy."
What ! has it not got tainted ? Has it not got
lowered now? Woe to those that say so! " The
faith " is just the same faith now as on the day of
Pentecost, the same faith that Peter preached, and
also Paul, and all others of the apostles. And we
have Peter and Paul, *i.e.* we have their words. We
have the most careful words they ever spoke. We
have the words that they were inspired to write
from God. We do not therefore merely listen, as
some of the early fathers talk about a man that
saw the apostle and heard the apostle ; and it
appears that the man that did so was a poor foolish
old man ! Very likely. Well, and what have you
got by putting a poor foolish old man between you
and the apostle ? Little or nothing. But Peter

and Paul and Jude were not foolish, and whatever
they may have been in themselves, there was the
mighty power of the Holy Ghost Who gave them the
truth of God absolutely intact ; and here it is His
word now, and we come into personal contact with
it by faith. We that believe receive that " most
holy faith," and what is more, we are called, every
one, to act upon it now.

And what are we to do with it ? It is not only
that we impart it to others, we " build up ourselves
on our most holy faith." Nothing, therefore, can
give a more delightful picture of the resources of
grace for as bad a time as can well be conceived as
what we have here. " Ye, beloved, building up
yourselves on your most holy faith " ; it is not to
be on a little bit of the faith, not on the faith that
was given to you through the intervention of a
poor foolish old man. No, here it is, fresh from God,
kept fresh and holy, unmixed with anything that
could lower it.

" Praying in the Holy Ghost." What can be
better than this ? There were men who spoke with
tongues in the Holy Ghost. Do you think that is
half as good as " praying in the Holy Ghost " ?
Why, the apostle Paul says that the men that spoke
with tongues in the Holy Ghost were to hold their
tongue, unless there were an interpreter there
present so as to give what they spoke in a tongue
in a form intelligible to others. It was a real power
of the Spirit of God, but it was not to be exercised

unless there were an interpreter. But think of the apostle silencing a man praying in the Holy Ghost ! No, the very reverse. There is a great deal of prayer that is not in the Holy Ghost. And we are not at all called upon only to pray in the Holy Ghost. Happy is he who does, and happy are they that hear prayer in the Holy Spirit. And where there is prayer in the Holy Spirit all is thoroughly acceptable to God, every word is so. Every word of such prayer expresses perfectly what God means at that time. But there are prayers that begin in the Spirit and do not end in the Spirit. Prayers are often rather mixed, and this is true even of real believers ; and sometimes we pray foolishly, sometimes we pray unintelligently ! This is never in the Holy Ghost.

And, what is more, we are encouraged to pray at all times, even supposing we say what is foolish. Very well, it is better to say it, than to be silent. Much better. Because prayer is the going forth of the heart to God, and it may be like the words of a prattling child to its father or mother. It is all right that the child should prattle, far better than that the child should be dumb. But the best of all is when it is really prayer in the Spirit of God ; yet that is a thing rather to desire than to presume that we have attained to. We have to be very careful indeed that we do not give ourselves credit for more activity in the Holy Ghost than we really possess. This supposes entire dependence, and no thought of self, and no opposition to this or to that.

These are things that, alas! may be, and they all weaken and hinder " praying in the Holy Ghost." But here you see the very same grace that encouraged the saints, even in the darkest day, " to build up themselves on their most holy faith," instead of having the notion, Oh, it is hopeless to look for that now ; when Peter or Paul was there we might have the most holy faith, but how could it be guaranteed now ? Well, there it is in this precious word. And those that cleave to this precious word will find it out, and if their heart is full of it, their mouth will abundantly speak of it ; and there is no ground to be discouraged, but the very contrary.

So, in this twentieth verse, we have two of the most important things possible—the one is, the standard of truth not in the least degree lowered, but maintained in all its highest and holiest character, even in that dark day ; and, the second, the most spiritual action that could be in any believer here below, viz., " praying in the Holy Ghost." Why, this is even more than preaching or teaching, because the heart is sure to be in the prayer. A man that can speak well and knows the truth—this may often be a snare. There is a danger in such a case to say the truth, and speak it out, and earnestly too, without there being present the power of the Spirit of God. But to pray in the Holy Ghost is another thing altogether. This cannot be without the immediate action of the Spirit in this most blessed way.

"Keep yourselves in the love of God." Here
Jude is looking at the practical result of these two
things. "Keep yourselves in the love of God."
Now, could we keep ourselves in anything better?
Was there ever anything higher than the keeping
ourselves in the love of God? Love is of God, and
we are to keep ourselves in it, instead of being
provoked by the evil things around us, instead of
yielding because of others yielding. This necessarily
supposes great confidence in God, and delight in
what God's own nature is—the activity of His
nature. Light is the moral character of God's
nature; love is the active character of God's
nature. Light does not allow any impurity; love
goes out to bless others. We are called to keep
ourselves, not merely in the light of God—we *are*
there, we are brought there as Christians—but, in
the love of God. We are not meant to have that
doubted. We are to keep ourselves fresh and
simple and confident in His love.

And he further adds, "Looking for the mercy of
our Lord Jesus Christ unto eternal life." I think
that mercy is brought in here especially because of
the great need, because of the distress, because of
the weakness, because of everything that tended to
cast people down. No, he says, do not be downcast,
look for the mercy of our Lord Jesus Christ. Is it
only by the way? No, it is all along the way, to the
very end—" unto life eternal," the great consummation. This could not be unless they already had

life eternal in Christ now ; but this mercy of God,
" of our Lord Jesus Christ unto life eternal," looks
at the full heavenly consummation.

VERSES 22, 23

Now we come to a passage which I feel to be
unusually difficult to expound ; and the reason is
this. The original authorities and the best authorities
are all in confusion about it. This is very rarely
the case in the New Testament, but it is the case
here. All the great authorities are at sixes and
sevens in the testimony they give of these two
verses (22, 23). And, to show you how great that
is, our Version—the Authorised, so-called—looks at
two cases only, " And of some have compassion,
making a difference "—that is one class ; " and
others save with fear, pulling them out of the fire ;
hating even the garment spotted by the flesh "—
this is the second class.

Now I believe there are three classes, and not two
only. That will show how uncertain it is. Although,
as I have said, I am very far from presuming to
give more than my judgment as far as the Lord
enables me to form one. I am certainly open to
anything that might be shown to the contrary, but
as yet no one has shown it.- No one at all. I think
that those who know best about it are those
that have spoken most cautiously as to it.

Many who trust themselves are apt to speak more confidently.

First of all Jude says, " And some convict when contending."* That is the idea—" when they dispute " ; not, " making a difference," as of the man that shows compassion. The fact is, compassion belongs to another class, not to this one at all, as far as I am able to judge, which depends upon looking at all the authorities and using one to correct another. That is what it comes to in this singular case, which is a very exceptional thing in the great original witnesses ; but God has been pleased in this particular instance not to hinder their difference.

Some then " convict when they dispute." I think that is the meaning of it. " Making a difference," as in the Authorised, should rather be, " when they dispute." It is the people that are being convicted who of course make the dispute, instead of the person that shows compassion making a difference among them. It is quite a different idea. The first class, in this twenty-second verse, has been given (in my belief) very wrongly indeed.

Well, then, the next is, instead of " convicting " people so as to leave them without any excuse for their disputatious spirit, another class is looked at— " others save, pulling them out of [the] fire " ; then,

* ἐλέγχετε AC*, the best cursives, and Vv., διακρινομένους ℵABC, good cursives, Vulg., Syrr., Arm.—Text. Rec. ἐλέειτε διακρινόμενοι KLP, etc.

a third class, " and others pity with fear*, hating even the garment spotted by the flesh " (ver. 23).

These then are the three classes : a disputatious class to be convicted and silenced—then, those that are to be saved, snatched out of the fire—and, others to be compassionated with fear, hating the garment spotted by the flesh. So that this all tends to complete the picture of the danger to souls. There is the all-importance of grace in the midst of it, but the truth maintained in all its power. And, you observe, it is for the same persons who are building up themselves on their most holy faith to do this. It is work that is thrown on the responsibility of those that were thoroughly happy and walking with God. These are the persons that would be able to silence the disputatious if they would be silenced by any one. But even apostles could not always do that. The apostle John speaks of the " malicious words " of Diotrephes. These words were directed against himself, and even an apostle could not alter that. The apostle Paul complained of " evil workers " who pretended to be quite as much apostles, if not more so, as himself. He refers to them in very trenchant terms in 2 Corinthians xi. He could not hinder that. And when there was the great meeting in Jerusalem, where all the apostles were present, there was a deal of disputation and

---

* σώζετε ἐκ πυρὸς ἁρπάζοντες ℵABC, best cursives, Vulg., Memph., Arm., Aeth., οὓς δὲ ἐλεᾶτε ἐν φόβῳ ℵA (ἐλεεῖτε) B, Vulg., Memph., Arm., Aethiop.—Text. Rec. ἐν φόβῳ σώζετε ἐκ τοῦ πυρὸς ἁρπάζοντες KLP, etc.

discussion there. It was only after it burst out in a
noisy meeting at first, that Peter, as well as Barnabas
and Paul, gave their testimony, and then James
summed up the decision of the assembly (Acts
xv.).

I only mention it to show that a like state of
things existed at that time as now. We often look
on the apostles as the painters represent the Lord.
If you look at the pictures of the Lord Jesus, He is
generally represented as going about with a halo of
glory about His head. Well, if that were true, one
might expect all the multitude to be down on their
knees looking up to the man with this golden halo
around him. But that is just what imagination
does. It puts a halo around the Lord, and it puts a
halo around the apostles ; so that people do not
realise at all the terrible evils that had to be faced
by them. This was the portion, too, of those that
were serving God, even in the best of times. How
much more may we expect it now ! As the Psalmist
said, Time was when the work of the sanctuary
was regarded as a good thing for a man to have
put his hand to : all that fine carved work, all that
grandeur of gold that gleamed in the sanctuary ;
but now it came to that pass, that a man was prized
because he brake it all to pieces (Ps. lxxiv.).

Well, this is what we have in the increasing
lawlessness of Christendom, but let us not be
downcast. Let us remember that the prize is
coming ; that the Lord puts especial honour on

those that are faithful to Him in an evil day. The Lord grant us that great privilege.

VERSES 24, 25

IN the body of the Epistle we have already had the coming of the Lord in judgment, that is to say, bound up in the awful departure from the truth which was to be found in the Christian profession. This is what many souls are very unwilling to face. It is natural for man to think that everything must be progressive—the truth as well as all else. No one ever drew that from the Bible, and every part of the Bible, from the first book till the last, shows us man set in a place by God, and abandoning it for Satan. And there is the same story here. No doubt it is unspeakably terrible to find that what bears the name of Christ should turn out worst of all. I need not say the guilt of it is entirely man's, and that the secret source of that evil is still Satan, as Satan is always behind the scenes in his antagonism, not only to God, but more particularly to the Lord Jesus. He is the One that Satan hates, and hates most of all because He became Man to glorify God where man had failed, and as Man to glorify God even about sin. Therefore, there is, what we might call, a natural antagonism in the devil, being what he is, against the One Who is to crush him at last. He well knows this, and there will come a time when, as he knows, he will have but a short time.

That time has not yet come, but it is coming, and coming fast.

So Jude introduces the coming of the Lord in a very remarkable manner—not by a new prophecy, but by the recovery to us of one of the first prophecies ever uttered, and, certainly, the first prophecy that took shape, the ordinary shape, which gave its character to all others that follow. For nothing could be more in the prophetic character than these words : " And Enoch also, the seventh from Adam (to distinguish him from the Enoch who was the son of Cain) prophesied of these, saying, Behold the Lord cometh with ten thousands of His saints, to execute judgment upon all, and to convince all that are ungodly among them of all their ungodly deeds, which they have ungodlily committed, and of (what people think little of) their hard words which ungodly sinners have spoken against Him." " Words " are the common expression of man's iniquity, because he cannot *do* all that he would like to do, but there is nothing he cannot " say." Consequently, it is said, " For by thy words thou shalt be justified, and by thy words thou shalt be condemned." This character of evil, so far from being a light thing, is one which is presented with the utmost gravity, and that by Enoch before the flood : and it is nowhere else preserved. Here, thousands of years afterwards, Jude was enabled to disclose this to us—by what means we do not know. The Holy Ghost was perfectly capable without using any means. Whether there were any, we know not, but we know that here it is, and that this is the certain truth, not only of God, but through Enoch before he went to heaven.

But there is another connexion with Enoch that we have now to look into, in the verses that close the Epistle. This is, that we may regard a latent connexion *in* them with the blessed manner in which Enoch was taken out of the scene altogether. Now, this fell to Jude and not to Peter. I have already compared the very great marks of distinction between Peter's and Jude's treatment of these very cases. Peter's view is purely as a question of unrighteousness, and he looks also at the teachers as being the most guilty parties in that unrighteousness—generally done for gain, or fame, or for some earthly motive of the kind that is not of God. Jude looks at it in a still deeper light ; for he does not make so much of the teachers. The awful thing to Jude was that the church, that the body of the saints, who ought to be the light of God—the heavenly light of God in a world of darkness—that they were to become the seat of the worst evil of Satan ; and this through letting in (no doubt, by carelessness, by lack of looking to God) these corrupters. That is his point of view. Not so much unrighteousness as apostasy. There is nothing so terrible as apostasy. In the case of unrighteousness it might be merely that of men going on with their badness. But apostasy always supposes that people have come out of their badness professedly, that they have received the truth professedly, that they have professedly received grace from God in Christ the Lord, and have turned their back upon it all. There is nothing so bad as that. So that you see, if there were not the gospel, and if there had not been the church, there could not have been so bad an apostasy as that which Jude contemplates here, from first to last.

We have, first of all then, as I have already shown, the trace of that apostasy as it presented itself to Jude by the Holy Ghost. And he takes his great figures of it from Israel, which after it was saved became the enemy of God, and fell under judgment. Peter does not say a word about that ; he looks at merely wicked men ; consequently, he is more occupied with the evil that brought on the deluge. Jude does not say a word about the deluge, because there was no question of a people being saved. There was a family—a few individuals— but there was not a people. Jude looks at the church, and compares the church getting wrong and losing everything after, having apparently gained everything : according to the picture of Israel, saved out of Egypt, and nevertheless, all coming to nothing.

We see how beautifully the figures employed and the illustrations used are all perfectly in keeping with the great differences between the two Epistles of Peter and Jude. And I mention it again, as I have already done, as a proof of the blindness of men in

our day, in what they call "higher criticism."
They will have it that the one Epistle is only a copy
of the other. Why, they are perfectly contrasted
the one with the other. There are some points, of
course, that must be common—the wickedness of
man, the grace of God, the truth of God. All that
must be common to the two Epistles.

But the character of the truth in the one case is
simply, men corrupting righteousness into unrighteousness—that is Peter. In Jude it is men, who were
blessed by the revelation of grace, turning it into
licentiousness, men who had not merely the authority
of God, but the authority of our Lord Jesus Christ.
Peter does not say a word about this. It is God's
authority. Even the Lord is there looked at as
Master—a Sovereign Master—not in the attitude
of "our Lord Jesus Christ." Jude adds that. So
Noah is the great figure in Peter ; whereas Enoch,
and not Noah, is the figure before us in Jude.

Now, I ask, how could the wit of man ever have
done this ? Even when people have read the two
Epistles, many Christians have not noticed these
differences, yet there they are. What learned men
see is the apparent resemblances between the two.
But that is an altogether unintelligent way of
reading anything. Because, even if you look at all
the men of the world, well, they all agree in being
men, but just think how foolish a person must be
who can see no difference between one man and
another because they are both men ! That is just

the way these learned men talk. They see no
difference between Peter and Jude, the one copied
the other ! Whereas the striking thing is that,
although they both go over the same ground, they
look at it in different ways—both full of instruction,
yet such instruction as only the Holy Ghost could
give.

Oh, how solemn when we read this last Epistle,
which bears upon the apostasy of Christianity, or
rather of Christendom, of those that were introduced
to the richest blessings of God's grace and truth in
Christ, yet turning to be the bitterest enemies of it
(not only abandoning it, but) treating it with
contempt and disdain, and with hatred to the last
degree.

This is exactly what we have in the middle of the
Epistle. We saw the characters that it takes,
particularly Cain, Balaam, and Korah—-the beginning, middle and end, I might say. The unnatural
brother that hated, not a mere man only, but his
own brother, and slew him. The bitterest enemies
of the faithful are always those who profess to be
faithful and are not. There is no bitterness so deep
as that of an unworthy bearer of the name of Christ.
Well, that is Cain. Not a word of this in Peter.
That belongs to Jude, and is here.

Then Balaam appears in Peter because he is a
false prophet that figures the false teachers, who
are more the thing in Peter, but not in Jude ; for
here it is the saints, the body of the saved ones—at

any rate in profession. That is what alarmed and shocked him. And he puts it forth for us, that we might now understand it, that we should not be too much perplexed by any of these terrible things which may break out at any time in our midst. There never was a more foolish idea, perhaps, entertained by some of us, that whoever might go wrong this could not happen amongst those called " Brethren." Oh, foolish Brethren, to flatter themselves in such a way as that ! Why you, we—for I take my place along with you in it altogether— we are the persons most liable to have the highest flown expressions and pretension to the greatest piety, while there may be an enormously evil thing going on. How are we to judge of such things ? By the word of God. And you will always find that those that are carrying on in that way slip from the word. They do not want the word. They want something new, something that will go on with the times, something that will make the " Brethren " more popular, something that will get bigger congregations, and all those things that are flattering to human vanity ; the consequence is they are naturally afraid of the word. No wonder. No one ever quarrelled with the word of God, if the word of God did not condemn them. Every person who loves the word owes to it all his entrance into blessing ; he derives all from that precious word and that precious word reveals Christ. Consequently we should not be occupied about pleasing others and

about their work, but with Christ. And we want all
God's children also to be occupied with Christ as
the only ground of any solid and sure peace.

In Enoch's prophecy we may observe once more
that it is not exactly " the Lord cometh," but,
" Behold, the Lord came." This manner of speaking
is quite usual in the prophets, and that is why they
are called " seers." What they described they saw
as in a prophetic vision. John saw all the various
objects which he describes in the Revelation. He
saw the heaven opened, and the Lord coming out,
and the throne set. But it does not mean that all
this was accomplished then. He saw it all before
it took place. So did Enoch. He saw the Lord
come ; and he presented it in that way. In Isaiah
liii. we see the same thing. " He is brought as a
lamb to the slaughter, and as a sheep before her
shearers is dumb, so He openeth not His mouth."
It does not mean that there was any doubt about
its being all future ; but that the prophet saw it
before his eyes, the eyes opened by the Holy Spirit.
It is the same thing here. The Lord is seen at the
close of the age coming with ten thousands of His
saints to take judgment, to inflict judgment on
these apostates ; and the Spirit of God here intimates
that the same family likeness of departure from
God has been going on since the days of Enoch,
and that it was to go on, not only in Jude's day,
but in the future till the Lord comes. It was all one
in character—hatred of God. And you see how

entirely this falls in with what I have been saying, that man always departs from God. It is not only that he is rebellious, not only that he behaves himself badly, not only that he violates this and that, but he turns his back upon God altogether and His truth. This is apostasy, and the spirit of it is already come. It will, come out thoroughly, and then the Lord will come in judgment.

But now the hope! What is that? Well, it is implied in what we saw. "Behold, the Lord came with ten thousands of His saints." The question is, How did they come with Him? If the Lord comes *with* His saints, He must have come before to fetch them to Himself, and this is just what He will do. But that is a thing entirely outside the prophetic introduction of the Lord's coming. The Lord's coming for His saints is not a matter of prophecy at all. It is a matter of love and hope; we may say of faith, love and hope. They are all in full play in the wonderful prospect that grace has opened out before our eyes. Therefore it is that the Lord does not introduce this prospect except in a very general way, in any of the Gospels so much as He does in John : " In My Father's house are many mansions : if it were not so, I would have told you. I go to prepare a place for you. And if I go and prepare a place for you, I will come again and receive you unto Myself " (John xiv. 2, 3).

There is nothing about prophecy in that passage. It is future, but its being future does not make it

prophecy. It is an abuse of terms to think that
prophecy is essentially bound up with judging a
wrong state of things and replacing it with a better.
But in this case, as in John xiv., the Lord, when
He comes to put us in the Father's house, does not
judge a wrong state of things. It is consummating
His love to the dearest objects of His love, not
merely on earth but for heaven ; and it is in that
way that the Lord speaks. It is the same thing in
the Revelation. After He has done with all the
prophetic part, He presents Himself as " the bright
and the morning star." And when the church has
that before her, we find a new thing, " The Spirit
and the bride say, Come." That is not prophecy ;
that is the church's hope, and it is strictly the
church's hope. Because when you say, " The Spirit
and the bride," it is not merely an individual, it is
the whole—personified—of the saints that compose
the bride. " The Spirit and the bride ! " What a
wonderful thing that the Spirit should put Himself
at the head of it ! " The Spirit and the bride say,
Come." It might have been thought, Oh ! that is
only a sanguine hope that the bride has got. But,
no ; you cannot talk about anything sanguine in
the mind of the Holy Spirit. " The Spirit and the
bride say, Come." Hence you see that the great
object of the Lord, in that close of the Revelation,
was to show that you must not mix up the hope of
the Lord's coming to receive us to Himself with the
accomplishment of prophecy. The hope is entirely

apart from any prophetic events. It is not in the seals, it is not in the trumpets, still less is it in the vials. It is after all these things that the Spirit of God, in the conclusory observations, gives there what the Lord had given, when Himself on earth, to His disciples. The Spirit of God takes up there what was suited to the then condition of the church. The church then knew that she was " the bride " of Christ. This had been clearly shown in more than one chapter of the Revelation. In chapter xix., the marriage of the Lamb had come, and the bride had made herself ready. That could not be the earthly bride. How could the earthly bride celebrate a marriage in heaven ? And how could the heavenly bride celebrate it there unless saints composing it had been taken there before ? This is just what I am about to come to.

Well, then, this coming of the Lord, which is " our hope," is exactly what Jude takes up here in the closing verses.

" But to Him that is able to keep you without stumbling, and to set you with exultation blameless before His glory ; to an only* God our Saviour through Jesus Christ our Lord† [be] glory, majesty, might, and authority, before all times,‡ and now, and unto all the ages. Amen " (vers. 24, 25).

* σοφῷ (wise) is omitted by ℵABC Vulg. Copt. Arm. Æthiop. and Syrr. Vv.—T.R. inserts with KLP and many cursives.

† διὰ Ἰησοῦ Χριστοῦ τοῦ κυρίου ἡμῶν ℵABCL Vulg. Copt. and Syrr. Vv.—T.R. omits with K.P.

‡ πρὸ παντος τοῦ αἰῶνος ℵABCL Vulg. Copt. Arm. and Æthiop. Vv.—T.R. omits with KP and most cursives.

"Now unto Him that is able to keep you from falling." How appropriate when thus presenting the dangers, the evils, the horrible iniquity of apostasy from all Christian grace and truth that might have the effect of greatly dispiriting a feeble soul ! No one ought even to be dispirited ; not one. "Now unto Him that is able to keep" clearly refers to every step of the way, and there is power in Him to keep. It is we who fail in dependence. Never does He fail in power to preserve. "Now unto Him that is able to keep you from falling and to present you faultless." Where ? "Before the presence of His glory." Where is that ? Is not that the very glory into which the Lord has now gone ? And does not He say, "that where I am there ye may be also " ? Here we find that the hope of the Christian and the hope of the church is entirely untouched by all the ruin that had come in. Spiritual power remained intact. And not only that : this glorious, blessed hope remains for our consolation and our joy in the darkest day.

"Now unto Him that is able to keep you without stumbling and to set you faultless before the presence of His glory with exceeding joy." There we have what falls in not with Peter, but with Jude. Jude, of course, entirely agrees with Peter, and confirms Peter as to the judgment that is to fall on those that were not only unrighteous but apostate. But then Jude does not forget that there are those that are true, that there are those that are faithful, that there are those that are waiting for Christ, that there are those that are even more appreciative of the blessing because of the unbelief of man. Therefore it is that he brings in this present power which depends entirely on the Holy Spirit's presence to keep us ; and, further, he speaks of the blessed hope depending upon Christ's coming to receive us to Himself, " and to present us faultless." That will only be because we are glorified ; that will only be because we are like Himself. He was the only One intrinsically faultless, and He is the One Who, by redemption, and then also by its accomplishment for the body—for redemption now is only as far as the soul is concerned, but when He comes it will be for the body as well—will present us faultless both in soul and body " before the presence of His glory with exceeding joy."

VERSE 25

" To the only [wise] God." The word "wise" has crept in here. In all correct texts the word " wise " disappears in this place. It is perfectly right in Romans xvi. 27. And I just refer to that text to show its appropriateness there : " To God only wise." I presume that it was this passage that led the ignorant monk, or whoever he was that was copying Jude, to (as he thought) correct it. But we cannot correct. All these human corrections are innovations, and our point is to get back to what

God wrote and to what God gave. Everything except what God gave is an innovation, but God's word is the standard, and all that departs from, or does without, it is an innovation.

Now, in this chapter of Romans, what made the word " wise " appropriate and necessary there, is that Paul refers to the mystery. He does not bring out the mystery in Romans; but after completing the great subject of the righteousness of God, first, in its personal application as well as in itself, secondly, comparing it with the dispensations of God, and, thirdly, in its practical shape—personal, dispensational, and practical—he here adds a little word at the close, " Now to Him that is of power to establish you according to my gospel, and the preaching of Jesus Christ, according to the revelation of the mystery." The revelation of the mystery— he had not brought this in. But he maintains that this gospel of his was according to it. It was not the revelation of it ; but it did not clash with it. There was no contrariety, but that revelation of the mystery was left for other Epistles, Ephesians and Colossians more particularly ; Corinthians also in a measure, but chiefly Ephesians and Colossians.

Further he says, " which was kept secret since the world began, but now is made manifest, and by prophetic writings " (or, scriptures, namely, those of the New Testament. I understand that what is called here " scriptures of the prophets " are the prophetic writings of the New Testament, of which

Paul contributed so much) " according to the commandment of the everlasting God made known to *all* nations "—that shows that the Old Testament prophets are not referred to here at all—" for obedience of faith ; to God only wise be glory." That is to say, this concealment of the mystery and now bringing it out in due time—not in Romans, but in what would be found to agree with Romans and confirm Romans when the mystery was com municated to the saints in the Epistles that had to be written afterwards—all this showed " God only wise." It is in connexion, you see, with this keeping back for so many ages, and now for the first time bringing out this hidden truth, the hidden mystery, as he calls it, to our glory, which is involved in Christ's exaltation at the right hand of God, and in His leaving the world for the time entirely alone, whilst meanwhile forming the disciples according to the truth of His being in heaven.

In Timothy, however, we have an expression exactly similar to what we have here. " Now unto the King eternal, immortal, invisible, the only God " (1 Tim. i. 17). There the word " wise " is brought in again in our Authorised Version. There is no reason for it there. So that there is the same error introduced in Timothy as there is in Jude, and both of them brought from what we already have in Romans xvi., where it ought to be. Here, we find again, what a dangerous thing it is for man to meddle with the word of God. The apostle is here

looking at God Himself, not at what He particularly
does. The wisdom of His revelation—that is in
Romans. But in Timothy it is, " Now unto the
King eternal, immortal, invisible, the only God."
There might be all these pretenders, these gods many
and lords many that Paul knew very well among the
Gentiles, and Timothy also, and particularly at
this very Ephesus where Timothy seems to have
been at this very time. There was the famous
temple (one of the wonders of the world), called the
temple of Diana. Artemis is the proper word, for
Diana was a Roman goddess, and Artemis was a
Grecian goddess quite of a different nature, although
there were kindred lies about the two.

Here, therefore, in Timothy the apostle presented
with great propriety and beauty " the only God."
Bringing in the " wise " God introduces quite
another idea which does not fall in with the context,
it does not agree with it properly. We find just the
same thing in Jude. So that the comparison, I
think, of the three scriptures will help to show that
" the only wise God " belongs to Romans ; that
" the only God "—Who is presented in contrast
with idols and imaginary beings—brings in to
Timothy the force of the " only " true God.

In Jude we have " the only God " for a slightly
different reason, but one equally appropriate. He is
looking at all this terrible scene and at the greatness
of the grace of God towards His beloved ones carried
through such an awful sea of iniquity and apostasy.

But if our eye be fixed on Christ, my dear brethren, it does not matter where we are, or whether we are smooth or rough. Some would make a great deal of the large waves, and I have no doubt that Peter was frightened at the big waves on which he found himself walking, and when he looked at the waves down he went. But if there had been no big waves, all as smooth as glass, and Peter had looked down on the glassy sea, down he would have gone all the same. It is not, therefore, at all a question of the particular circumstances. The fact is, there is no power to keep us, except a divine one, and it is all grace ; and the grace that supports on a smooth sea is equally able to preserve on a rough one. Whatever, therefore, may be the special characters of evil and of danger at the present time, all turns upon this : What is Christ to my soul ? And if I believe in His grace and in His truth then what does not my soul find in Christ ?

" Now, unto Him that is able to keep you from falling, and to present you faultless before the presence of His glory, with exceeding joy." For the grace on His part is just the same as if there had been no departure, no apostasy, no wickedness, no unrighteousness of any kind. He wrought His marvellous work of grace for us when we were nothing but sinners. He brought us to Himself when we were no better—unmoved, perhaps, by that wonderful work when we first read and heard about it. But when the moment came for us to

believe on Him, how it changed all ! And surely
the times that have passed over us have only
endeared the Lord more to us. I hope there is not
a soul in this room but what loves the Lord a deal
better to-day than the day on which he, or she, was
first converted. It is one of those notions of
Christendom that our love is always much better
and stronger on the day we were first converted.
Never was there greater mistake. There was a
feeling of mercy, no doubt ; a deep sense of pardon-
ing grace, but, beloved friends, do we not love the
Lord for incomparably more than what we knew
when converted ? Surely that love has grown with
a better knowledge of His love, and of His truth.
And here we find that His grace is exactly the
same, that the grace that brought Him from heaven,
the grace of Him, Who lived here below, that died
here below, and is now gone back into glory, is
without change ; and that the exceeding joy or
exultation will be unquenched in the smallest degree
when the blessed moment comes. " He will set us
blameless before the presence of His glory, with
exceeding joy." It is not very much to find where
the exceeding joy is. I am persuaded it is both in
Him and in us. Perhaps we may be allowed to say,
" which thing is true in Him and in you " (1 John
ii. 8). That was said about another thing altogether
—the love that He put into our hearts when we
knew His redemption ; for until we know redemption
there is not much love in a believer. He may have

a good bit of affection for the people that he is intimate with, but he is very narrow at first, and till he knows the love of Christ his affections do not at all go out to all the saints. Here then we find, at any rate, this glowing picture of that bright hope, when it will surely be accomplished.

Now, Jude adds, " To the only God." For who could have met all this confusion ? Who could have conceived and counselled all this grace and truth ? Who could have kept such as we are through all, remembering our total weakness, our great exposure, the hatred of the enemy, the contempt of adversaries, of all that are drawn away, of all the enticement to go wrong, all the animosities, worst of all, created by any measure of faithfulness ? Yet He does keep through it all. " The only God our Saviour " ; not only Christ our Saviour. Christ is the accomplisher of it all, but here Jude looks at God as the source, and it is no derogation from Christ. It was the delight of Christ on earth to present God as a Saviour God, and not merely that He Himself was that personal Saviour, the Son of man. So here the apostle desires that we should ever honour God our Saviour, as indeed we find it rather a common expression in those very solemn Epistles to Timothy.

" To the only God our Saviour." All other dependence is vain, all other boast is worthless. We are intended to rejoice, or, rather more strictly, to " boast in God through our Lord

Jesus Christ, by Whom we have now received the
reconciliation."

" To [the] only God our Saviour, through Jesus
Christ our Lord, be glory, majesty, might and
authority, before all time, and now and ever (or, to
all the ages)." It is a very interesting thing to note
here the propriety with which Jude closes the
Epistle. He says, " Be glory, majesty, might and
authority, before all time, and now, and for ever-
more, Amen." He looks at the full extent of
eternity. It is much more precise than what we
have in our Authorised Version ; and is here given
according to the reading of the best authorities,
and rightly adopted by the Revisers.

Peter also closes his Second Epistle in what is
said to be the same. But there is this distinction,
that whilst Peter speaks of " glory both now and
unto eternity's day " (iii. 18), Jude brings out in the
remarkable completeness of his closing ascription
what was, and is, and is to be, in all its full eternal
character.